The Human Factor

THE

HUMAN

FACTOR

Management Culture in a Changing World

Rolf W. Habbel

First published 2002 by
PALGRAVE MACMILLAN
Houndmills, Basingstoke, Hampshire RG21 6XS and
175 Fifth Avenue, New York, N.Y. 10010
Companies and representatives throughout the world

PALGRAVE MACMILLAN is the global academic imprint of the Palgrave
Macmillan division of St. Martin's Press, LLC and of Palgrave Macmillan Ltd.
Macmillan® is a registered trademark in the United States, United Kingdom
and other countries. Palgrave is a registered trademark in the European
Union and other countries.

ISBN 1–4039–0195–3 hardback

This book is printed on paper suitable for recycling and made from fully
managed and sustained forest sources.

A catalogue record for this book is available from the British Library.

Library of Congress Cataloging-in-Publication Data

Habbel, Rolf.
    The human factor : management culture in a changing world / Rolf Habbel.
        p. cm.
    Includes bibliographical references and index.
    ISBN 1–4039–0195–3
        1. Business planning. 2. Human capital—Management. 3. Employee
    empowerment. 4. Decentralization in management. I. Title.

HD30.28 .H268 2002
658.3'15—dc21   2002070644

Translation by Iain Grant

Editing and origination by Aardvark Editorial, Mendham, Suffolk

10   9   8   7   6   5   4   3   2   1
11   10   09   08   07   06   05   04   03   02

Printed and bound in Great Britain by
Creative Print & Design (Wales), Ebbw Vale

CONTENTS

This book is not intended to offer a template for the successful manager in the 21st century. It is about the personality of management, where the human dimension is a natural measure of how that personality acts. There are no formulae or seminars for this human dimension. The book foregoes cheap and easy suggestions from the repertoire of standard methods in the management literature, and does not seek to adopt the tone of the all-knowing management guru. The job of the top manager is too serious for this – and the author has too great a respect for the leading figures of the economy.

This book is based on the deep and fundamental conviction that the thinking and actions of the top manager must be legitimised in ethical terms, and that the status of any leadership figure within the economy can ultimately be assessed by whether he or she satisfies this requirement for legitimacy, notwithstanding the primacy of the success criteria and performance data. Taking this conviction as its starting point, this book is not only informed by decades of experience gathered from the practice of a globally operating consultancy partnership, but also draws on and gives significant weighting to the insights and opinions of top managers from various sectors of the economy, gathered in intensive discussions.

Observation and evaluation are set out with suitable differentiation between the two, along the lines of the altruistic thinking required of the manager by the Jesuit Professor Rupert Lay.[1]

In a corporate context, is the people factor simply a cost factor which really cannot be afforded, or at best afforded only when business is going

very well? And, if you ask the opinion of an honest salesperson, when has that ever been the case? Or is the people factor a priori a success factor? The answer cannot be a simple yes or no. The human factor, in the thinking and actions of the entrepreneur, has as many different facets as there are causes for success. However, the reverse conclusion is certainly true: where employees within a company feel they are treated 'without humanity' (by which I mean unfairly or unjustly, not impartially), or where a sense of negativity pervades the factors contributing to the social functioning of the company, then there can be no expectation of lasting economic success. But if fairness and justice – perhaps it would be more accurate to use the term 'objectivity' – can be defined as an essential criterion in determining whether or not a manager is demonstrating the human factor in his or her actions, then it immediately becomes easier to develop a useable, sufficiently generally applicable profile of requirements for the manager who has a feel for the people factor and how to act accordingly. One can then consider how this requirement profile measures up against the vital challenges facing top managers at the start of the 21st century.

On the other hand, the question about the human factor as a cost factor does not appear, at first sight, to have been simply plucked out of the air – and particularly if the question is asked in this way without any differentiation and without reflection. The 'costs of the people factor' are, if properly applied, investments in the smooth or, more realistically, more conflict-free, conduct of business. That may sound cynical to socio-romantic ears, but it is not meant cynically, for a company which is managed to take account of the people factor is in no way a subsidiary of the welfare state which is committed to (or should that be trapped by?) a claims-based mentality; rather, it is an economic, profit-oriented organisation, where people feel comfortable and therefore make their own contribution to the company's success of their own free will and out of their own self-motivation, thus having a just share in this success. Rupert Lay's opinion on this question is wholly unambiguous: 'One occasionally hears it denied that the highest goal of a business is to optimise profits. For the most part that is hypocrisy, or an otherworldly philanthropy.'[1]

On the basis of the diverse wealth of experience which a corporate consultant gathers through many years of collaborating with organ-

isations undergoing change, this book attempts to make the connections between the major global trends, which lead to constant change in the framework conditions for the economy and economic activity, and the key entrepreneurial challenges and success factors. The book seeks to elaborate and demonstrate that the individual – often all too easily overlooked as a 'small cog', given the scale of new management methods and concepts – is becoming increasingly decisive in determining whether a company is successful in managing this change. Against this background, the book then attempts to set out a CEO agenda with wider applicability, taking management with the people factor as its core element.

The company which is managed to take account of the human factor, in particular, gets its vitality from the performance of its employees. This performance will be all the greater if the employees feel that their work is justly valued and appropriately recognised. For that reason, the objectivity of the manager is a key element in his or her conduct, in order to provide that people factor. Objectivity makes the manager's thinking and actions understandable. The individual employee will support many developments if he or she can rely on the fact that there are no biased preferences influencing these changes. The person who can live out this ideal is trusted over many issues – even where the matters involved are not always easy to accept. In order for those in the company to support developments, there is also a need for comprehensible communication of decisions and change processes. The ability to communicate has a high priority in the list of requirements for the 21st-century manager. If management does not succeed in convincing its employees that the company is on the right track, that it has a long-term future, that it must innovate to secure that future and that ultimately it depends on its customers for its existence, then in the long term that company has no chance of being successful.

If one follows this line of thinking, one arrives at the inescapable conclusion that the human factor is a basic precondition for a successful business. This book demonstrates the ways to achieve successful working with the people factor.

At this point, I would like to thank all those who have contributed to the realisation of this book: alongside Booz Allen Hamilton, the international management and technology consultancy, which has given me the opportunity over 20 years to gather valuable experiences in strategic

processes, transformation processes and management processes, particular thanks are due to Alfred Lambeck, who has not only enriched me through our personal discussions, but also made a decisive contribution to the realisation of this book through his intensive collaboration on the thinking behind it, and also to Sabine Deuschl who supported the author with research and coordination of the whole book project. Above all, however, my thanks must go first and foremost to my wife and family, who have always supported me unselfishly and with understanding for the fact that on occasions there was less time available for them.

CHAPTER 1

In a World of Change

1.1 Globalisation: A Revolution in Scale

It would probably be an exaggeration to say that the thought of globalisation fills most people with feelings of enthusiasm. Rather, the
prospect of living in a global village makes many people feel uncom-
fortable in the face of what is unfamiliar. The former mayor of Stuttgart,
Manfred Rommel, articulated this feeling of discomfort towards the
supposed threat represented by the new scale of things in a brief but
double-edged story: 'There was once a man who wanted to buy a globe.
After inspecting the various models, he came to the conclusion that he
would be quite happy with a globe of Germany.'[2] I believe that this tale
should not only provoke us to respond with the wry smile of those in the
know, but should also be a cause for reflection among a thinking audience. Generally, individuals do not like to be stripped of their surroundings, and required to reorient themselves on a global scale instead of
going about their business confidently in a familiar setting. Countering
the challenges of globalisation with a human scale is proving to be an
issue all too easily forgotten in the rush towards the new global dimensions – especially when managers forge ahead in the seven-league boots
of megamergers.

  Globalisation is not a business objective which can be freely chosen,
such as growth, diversification or quality awareness, but is an intellectual and technological revolution with world-encompassing dimensions
that no one can escape. Globalisation means a departure from geographical, cultural and mental borders – borders which are being overcome

with the help of new thinking on a global scale, in a manner which is only now possible through modern information and communications technologies. These technologies consign national and continental boundaries to a past age. Notwithstanding all the technological expansions to the scope and the speed of management decisions, for almost all other change processes the following holds true: globalisation begins in people's heads.

To express it somewhat poetically, globalisation is a fruit of peace; it has thrived in a long period of what is at least relative peace between peoples. And it has increased in dynamism, tempo and scope following the end of the Cold War and the collapse of authoritarian systems with their ponderous, centrally controlled economies. DaimlerChrysler CEO Jürgen Schrempp even takes this view a stage further: 'Globalisation is not creating new conflicts, but is a key to realising peace.'[3]

The Triumph of Superior Systems

Political and economic action on a global scale presupposes both global thinking and well-developed information systems. Of course, this is not something which has only been recognised on the cusp of the third millennium; it was equally known to the Caesars of Rome, in the context of their world, just as to the Tsars of the Russian Empire or the strategists in the Pentagon during the Gulf War. The road and messenger system in Roman times, the telegraph lines across the kingdom of the Tsars which were put up by Werner von Siemens, and the digital information and communications systems used by General Norman H. Schwarzkopf – in their own time, each of these systems was a precondition for superiority and triumph. Schwarzkopf's book *It Doesn't Take a Hero*[4] demonstrates that 'Desert Shield' and 'Desert Storm' were battles of the telephony systems for the commanders in chief, and that the better communications systems played a key role.

The wire-based telephone network which spanned the globe, with all the shortcomings of the pre-satellite era, had already been hailed, rightly, as the largest machine in the world. But it was only in the last decades of the 20th century that the users of this machine began to imagine the true potential and scope of this 'machine' and the oppor-

tunities which it offered, against a background of the enormous acceleration and expansion of capacities as a result of digitisation, satellites and fibreoptic cabling.

Digitisation, deregulation, satellite technologies, the Internet, e-Business and mobile phones/m-Commerce are all motors of progress which have generated powerful driving forces and which will continue to develop for a long time. One only needs to think of the latest generation of mobile phones, offering effortless, if still limited, Internet access. Convergence is the keyword for new scales of development. The 'global player' is characterised by the fact that he or she knows how to harness these driving forces to realise growth for his or her own business. The Internet intensifies and accelerates this process, as it makes it possible for everyone, even the small producer, to find customers everywhere on the planet.

Motivating People to Have the Courage to Take a New Direction

Globalisation is seen by forward-thinking managers as an opportunity, rather than a threat. There is no doubt, however, that this opportunity involves major challenges for top management; and of these, the greatest challenge is clearly that of winning people over to have the courage to take that new direction along with management. Rational arguments alone will not be enough to bring this about. Globalisation presents the challenge of taking a determined approach to the processes of necessary structural adaptation. Of necessity, it demands decentralised corporate structures in which staff have confidence (see sections 2.3 and 2.4). It goes without saying that these market-facing units must therefore be provided with the necessary ability and authority to take decisions, in order to allow the necessary space to follow thinking through and take action once they have been motivated in support of the new direction.

The globally active business of the future works with local and regional units, which are customer-oriented and therefore largely independent, and with a global core, a head office which is reduced to and concentrated on the indispensable central functions of the business. In

terms of both functions and working methods, the CEO heading up such a globally networked organisation differs considerably from the inherited image of the traditional chairman of the board, looking down from his desk on the highest floor of the main administrative offices onto the production operations he commands. The radical nature of the transformation in corporate structures will hardly be less than that of the change and expansion in the thinking of the company management, brought about through globalisation, which triggers the transformation process.

Global Strategies and a Deep Understanding of Local Specificities

Global activities with a local presence, including in the area of production, often call for flexible extended enterprise structures as a matter of course, for example to bring in local suppliers and high-performance logistics companies, who contribute on the one hand to improved customer satisfaction, and on the other hand to minimising inventory volumes which tie up capital.

One fascinating aspect of these developments lies in the fact that global strategies can only be realised through a local presence and with a deep understanding for local specificities. At the same time, it should be acknowledged that the diversity of local markets with all their different forms does not facilitate the formulation of a consistent and internationally effective strategy in any way. Telecommunications and information technologies are indispensable aids in the development of a global presence, but they are only tools. As the phrase implies, only those companies who possess a worldwide sales network can be called global players. A corporate presence which is the same worldwide, being the expression of corporate identity, demands – and I cannot emphasise this point strongly enough – careful adaptation to local culture, the local mind-set and local peculiarities. In any given location, however, this correlation is secured in the first instance through the people and employees, through the corporate partners and of course through the customers on the ground. Anyone who ignores this aspect is all too likely to come to grief. Helmut Maucher, the successful ex-chairman of the board at Nestlé, has remarked on the challenges which this presents for managers:

Anyone who does not understand other cultures, who is incapable of thinking internationally, who is not open to outside influences and who only operates in his own national or regional environment, will have difficulties.[28]

Understanding cultures means accepting that regional characteristics are the assets of the European Community today, and these may possibly persist in a strengthened form if one's 'homeland' in Europe is in future no longer defined by country borders, but by regions sharing a consciously preserved cultural unity.

Preserving Cultural Identity – Respecting Difference

Companies which, in the context of globalisation, fail to respect such cultural, and therefore deeply human aspects are passing up major opportunities. Incidentally, Maucher believes that this is:

One of the problems which the Americans have, even though they set the tone and are leading the way. However, their country is so large that they have difficulty in understanding people who have a different way of life, a different culture, or different consumer behaviour.[28]

On the other hand, companies based in small countries – such as Nestlé in Switzerland; Philips in the Netherlands; ABB, Electrolux and Ericsson in Sweden; and Nokia in Finland – recognised at an early stage that they could only achieve significant size through internationalisation and ultimately globalisation of their activities. The results of this insight are known to all. As national and cultural identity play a major role especially in these smaller countries of origin, it was a lot easier for these businesses and their managers to respect the different nature of other countries and other markets.

At the Booz Allen Hamilton Employers' Forum 1999, Hans Konradin Herdt described the global market for goods and services as the natural biotope for the new phenomenon of the 'World plc'. Herdt countered this new organisation with journalistic scepticism:

At best, the World plc exists in a virtual sense. It no more exists than does a Société Anonyme Monde or a World Incorporated. There is not even a

Europe plc, no matter how incessantly the debate may rage about its existence. The prospects for the success of these efforts are known, and they are depressing. Even the pilot project represented by DaimlerChrysler is not a World plc. Frankly, it is a joint-stock company under German law with dual company offices in Stuttgart and in Auburn Hills. On that basis, it is above all a bilateral arrangement, in the way that Royal Dutch Shell and Unilever were a long time ago. To that extent, the World plc is actually a European invention. But of course we all know what is meant by the impressive image of the World plc.[5]

Klaus von Dohnanyi, former first mayor of Hamburg, spoke at the Booz Allen Hamilton Employers' Forum 1995 and addressed a very interesting aspect of internationalisation and globalisation. He pointed out the difficulty of forming majorities, and thus majority opinions or majority decisions, in supranational political forums and institutions. In the national context, and when counting votes within limited areas, it is possible to arrive at clear majorities. If one attempts to translate these procedures for forming a democratic majority to Europe and less tightly delineated areas, then the quantities of votes and thus the majorities can no longer be read clearly. As a result, even the decisions become unclear. There is a close analogy with large corporations operating across national boundaries, which have perhaps also completed a number of company mergers within a short period of time. Even appointing the CEO and his or her team becomes considerably more difficult than for a company operating in a national framework, as a number of different supervisory committees then have a say in proceedings, and these may be working to completely different objectives. When a CEO such as Jürgen Schrempp was appointed by 'his' German supervisory board, the whole affair was a far more straightforward matter, notwithstanding the aspect of employee co-determination (as required under German law), than if it were to involve the supervisory board and employees of a globally operating company such as Daimler-Chrysler, which is subject to a range of influences. In such corporations with a claim to global player status, it is harder to understand where the majority lies, and the relationships sustaining that majority are more difficult to manage. Problems like these call for new solutions in keeping with the borderless world of the economy.

Concern for the Preservation of Social and Ethical Standards

Reservations about globalisation are not justified by citing problems such as these, however, but above all by voicing concern over the standards for ecologically and socially responsible entrepreneurial thinking and actions. The fear is that these generally accepted standards, as developed by the social partners on both sides of industry, could be aligned downwards to fit with the lower standards of the less developed countries, rather than the reverse being the case. The fact that ideologically constrained viewpoints also play a part in this argument, as was the case in the debate about multinational corporations where the argument was considered won a long time ago, does not completely diminish the legitimacy of this feeling of unease. In the lecture which has already been quoted, Herdt took issue with these recurring critics:

> Because everyone can see it happening and it can therefore easily be used to support an argument, does it mean that the global wave of company mergers (which long ago spilled over into the Federal Republic of Germany) is creating a breeding-ground for a new critique of capitalism, targeting 'turbo-capitalism' or 'pure capitalism'? Spectres are haunting the stage, being labelled neo-liberal – with the word neo-liberal being devalued in much the same way as the word conservative was in the past, to become simply a protestor's cliché.

Globalisation includes the problem of industrial and commercial activity in different cultures, which need to be respected in their difference. Attempts at equalising differences, with more or less ill-considered interventions in the existing social framework at that point, without consideration for the people affected, are condemned to failure, whether in highly developed industrial countries or in developing countries. The entrepreneurial achievement in globally active companies lies precisely in adapting to the differentiated conditions through decentralised, largely self-governing market-facing units, and at the same time establishing the legitimacy of the binding common canon of values applied in daily actions on the ground.

> Lasting growth can only be achieved if companies make a visible and acknowledged contribution to the economic, social, and also ecological stability of those countries where they operate and work[3]

is how Jürgen Schrempp formulates this point, in his 'Ten Theories on Globalisation'. Understood in this way, globalisation assumes a significant ethical, human perspective. Rationality, justice, appropriateness, human dignity and fairness are the quality criteria for the application of the profit principle, suitable for the context and the manner in which profit is generated.

1.2 The I-World: At Home In Virtual Worlds

From a position of fascinating proximity, we are currently experiencing the rapid realisation of the I-World – that new, globally networked world of business in our information society which presents management with completely new challenges. The potential of the Internet to connect people and businesses all around the world with one another is not that different from the potential offered by the telephone. But the effects, particularly on the world of business and on mankind in both the private and professional spheres, will be far more wide-reaching. Furthermore, these effects have already developed at a pace unprecedented in the history of the development and dissemination of new technologies. It took the telephone 38 years to reach the level of the first ten million users, and, although the mobile telephone and the PC were the most rapidly disseminated technologies, nevertheless, it still took seven years before ten million users had access to a PC. However, with the Internet, four years were sufficient to achieve this significant milestone and to go beyond it at a phenomenal pace. With the information society as the determining engine of growth driving development forward, the telecommunications industry is currently growing remarkably faster than the global economy. The primary sector has overcome its decline from the start of the industrial age to the present day. As we enter the 21st century, the industrial sector, and the retail and services sector are showing only slight signs of continued fall-off, now that they have 'become attuned' to conditions. By contrast, even

though the information sector is presently in a phase of rather slow development, it is at the start of a rapid climb, which may possibly only level off again towards the end of this century. Allied to the extraordinary pace of development of the I-World is a second challenge for management, one which represents an even greater challenge in terms of its direct effects: one of the radical changes, reaching into every corner of business life, is the ever-increasing speed of all business processes. If the pace of business life is fast today, then in the digital age it will accelerate dramatically. Product life-cycles have shortened from years to months. Demand for completely new services develops at lightning speed. Decisions are expected to be made in real time. In the USA, 'hyperspeed' is a buzz word. It is unlikely to remain limited to the USA.

The results of a survey of top managers around the world reveal a completely new picture of the world of business, and of the I-World in the third millennium. Dr Gerd Wittkemper, Senior Partner at Booz Allen Hamilton, summarises the findings:

> Companies are changing from the bottom up to remain competitive in the digital age. Many of them will put in place a fundamentally new business system. In doing so, business models which have been around since the start of the industrial age over 200 years ago will for the first time no longer be applicable. A new world of business is being created – the I-World.[6]

It calls into question experiences and forms of organisation and marketing relating to business life which have been valid for decades, and forces management to develop new business forms – and to do all this at a speed which was wholly unimaginable even a decade ago, as the pace continues to accelerate. As a result, continuity and the anchoring of core corporate values are becoming of central importance.

Europe Must Catch Up with Regard to the Internet

A signal of the intensity and speed of this development can be seen in the creation of 1.2 million qualified jobs in the US Internet industry in 1998. No other technology has ever penetrated the market so quickly. In less

than five years, more than ten million households were reached. And in no other area of economic life have so many people found in so short a space of time not only a job and a way to make a living, but attractive professional work which enhances the prospects for their personal future. This fact remains untouched by the rapid economic slowdown in 2001/2002. Currently the USA dominates Internet business and the use made of the Web by its users. As a result, the Internet has so far had its strongest influence and effect on the North American economy. The extent to which North America provides the development of the Internet with both a focus and with potential can be seen from a single fact: in 1997, 53 per cent of all Internet users were based in the USA. In 2001, that figure had only dropped to 47 per cent. The American share of global Internet business is even higher, at 82 per cent. As early as the end of 1998, over 20 per cent of households had an Internet connection and a third of these were already making purchases via the Internet.

For me, actual examples give better proof than abstract figures of the level of economic importance achieved by e-Business in the USA by 1999:[54]

- Dell Computers, competing against Compaq and IBM to be number one in the global PC market, was selling PCs with a value of more than $35 million every day via the Internet. In 1999, that already represented around 43 per cent of total Dell sales.

- Cisco, one of the leading manufacturers of Internet infrastructure providing positive forecasts again, after a slowdown in 2001, was already conducting close on 70 per cent of its business via the World Wide Web.

- A good quarter of all share-dealing in the USA was taking place via the Internet – with the trend increasing.

- Amazon.com, the first and still the largest Internet (book) retailer, had achieved more than 10 million customers.

- One in four car-buyers were making use of the Internet before deciding which car to buy, or to make a direct purchase. In the USA, 80 per cent of people were using the Internet to gather information before making a purchase.

Close on a third of top managers in North America believe that the Internet has already had a major effect on the market, but 90 per cent are forecasting that the Internet will have a dominant or highly influential impact on the market within the next three years. Even though the time horizon may have changed in the meantime, this trend remains unchanged. According to a comprehensive study initiated by Booz Allen Hamilton and carried out jointly with the Economist Intelligence Unit, the expectations of the 600 CEOs interviewed were directed very strongly towards those changes brought about by the Internet: one third of them expect that the Internet will force their business to change its strategies and 59 per cent also assume that at the same time Internet technologies will help them to achieve their strategic goals. (Incidentally, European managers voice the same expectations, in almost identical percentages.)

The managers interviewed named the following points as the most important strategic priorities to be achieved with the help of the Internet:

- Improving customer satisfaction (78 per cent)

- Cost reductions (77 per cent)

- Globalisation of their business activities (62 per cent)

- Encouraging innovation (55 per cent).

In addition to this, North American managers expect that through using the Internet and its technologies, their companies can:

- Achieve better collaboration internally and externally

- Become more responsive and flexible than before

- Achieve greater cohesiveness in terms of committing staff to the company

- Achieve greater globalisation.

They also believe that through this process a better and more profound understanding of common tasks will develop; it will be possible to take decisions more quickly; and, as a result of the better flow of information,

employees would be more highly motivated to apply themselves actively to corporate goals. European managers express the same expectations in these areas too, and in percentage terms their answers barely differ from the North American responses.

Creating Room for Manoeuvre – Treating People as People

The range of activities undertaken by the creative workers, by the new brokers of the I-World, by the knowledge workers operating on an interdisciplinary basis, will extend in future from system integration through to the knowledge market on the Internet. It is sufficiently important to restate it here: businesses will only be successful if they can combine their knowledge network and their ability to connect knowledge with the ability to lead people, to enthuse people with their ideas, and to treat the people who lie behind the knowledge as people. Helmut Maucher has made an insightful comment on this relationship:

> The more we work with computers, with the Intranet and the Internet, the more the risk increases that the whole thing becomes something abstract and no longer human.[28]

Put in positive terms, this means that those companies which do not lose their sense of the people factor when working with the I-World have the best chances of being successful.

It is not only roles and functions which will change, but whole sectors and their familiar boundaries. Customers and suppliers all around the world can be reached via the new portals on the Internet. Employees in modern businesses use a 'workplace portal' to reach everything they need for their work – either from within their own company, or from others via the Internet or Intranet. This makes it immaterial whether they have their place of work at the company office, in the traditional style, or at home. Accordingly, in the next 10–15 years it is likely that around a third of all office-based staff will work from home on two of their five working days. That even applies to specialist staff working on research and development projects.

The second major and all-encompassing effect of the I-World again stands out here: the – I am tempted to add the word 'merciless' – speed, which will continue to increase and to which people in the world of business will have to adapt. Whatever they may have signified in the past, boundaries have become obsolete. The Internet facilitates the exchange of information, evaluations and knowledge at a pace which is of a wholly new order. Whether it is a job application or a business consultancy, whether customers are being won or lost, the Internet has an accelerating influence on these and on an almost unlimited number of other processes.

e-Business Gains Importance

Regardless of the setback in 2001, new forms of advertising and marketing – such as those connected with developments in e-Business – have been, and will be, spreading via the Internet (for which the volume of turnover in Europe has already exceeded €7.7 billion in 1999). It has taken barely two years for nearly all major businesses to attempt to establish a presence in the e-Business market – even if the path to economic success (for which read profit) remains a distant prospect. To put it another way, the I-World is demanding far faster management responses and decisions, and it is demanding them at speeds which are beyond the scope of traditional organisational and decision-making structures. This process only becomes critical if, given this increase in pace, there is a threat that the human aspects of the process will become lost. However, this does not have to be the case. Speed ultimately also means saving time. Saving time can also mean gaining the time to pause for breath amidst the hurly-burly of business life, time for individual discussion. Despite this, one's individual/personal network will still be important, but it will be more knowledge-based and therefore even richer.

Speed can also exact a price, just as it does for high-performance sportspeople, racehorses and Formula One racing drivers. They burn out quickly – and what happens then? Observers are agreed that the best prospects for e-Business are in the area of business-to-business (B2B) dealings. In mid-1997, Forrester Research were forecasting B2B turnover volume of a maximum of $327 billion for 2002 in the USA. In

1999, the prediction for 2002 was adjusted upwards to $1.3 trillion.[49] Possibly this was too optimistic. Businesses are looking at significant potential for cost reductions. Whether these cost reductions are to benefit the respective ordering company or the supplier is still an open question today. At the same time, companies are envisaging major opportunities to improve customer satisfaction thanks to faster and more error-free order and delivery processes.

By contrast, Internet trade with private customers initially appears to be flourishing, mainly for books and CDs, and increasingly for the marketing of music titles in MP3 mode – a procedure whereby the desired title is instantly downloaded from the Internet onto the home PC. A necessary consolidation process has already begun. In other sectors the experiences have not (yet?) been so favourable, because here the initial costs of marketing and advertising can only be recouped with larger volumes and more sustained customer commitment. However, it is precisely this readiness to commit to a supplier which is the sticking point for Internet shoppers, who are predominantly in the younger age groups. Incidentally, psychological factors are also in play here, and their importance is likely to increase further with better education and correspondingly more considered purchasing behaviour. In terms of his mind-set, the customer buying mail-order goods from high-quality retailers could possibly be the most likely to become an e-Commerce user, if he is young and adaptable enough and if he is approached with a convincing marketing strategy – one example being the mail-order operation Otto Versand. This Hamburg-based mail-order company was able to raise its Internet turnover for 1999 to DM100 million, a three-fold increase on the previous year. Group Chairman Michael Otto anticipates that by 2005 Internet turnover will make up around ten per cent of total turnover. Otto does not believe that the Internet will entirely supplant other avenues for marketing: Internet selling supplements other sales channels.[55] The Internet portals play an important role, being consumer-friendly access routes to the Internet via which the consumer can arrive at a multitude of offers in comfort and using only a few mouse-clicks. Yahoo!, one of the best-known and most successful Internet-based portals, is in the process of completing its conversion to become a media house, offering content while constantly expanding its core services.

The universities and business schools in the USA are already reacting decisively to the new requirements of the I-World, and far more significantly than is the case in Europe. Graduates in economics, business and management, the law and the political sciences coming out of our universities are not yet routinely equipped with the full breadth of computer skills which they must have in order to be successful. Frequently, graduates are acquiring these skills on work placements, as they gather their first experiences of industry. Many also take the self-study route in acquiring these skills successfully. Confident handling of computer-based knowledge, used as an aid to working which is as much routine as it is indispensable, is still far from being a skill which everyone possesses, and particularly so when thinking about management personnel already in post. It must become a matter of course to view and use the computer and its modern derivatives, such as the PDA (personal digital assistant), as a tool – of this I am convinced. This way of seeing things cannot begin early enough, and certainly it should start well before university level. It must be part of the core thinking in school that the computer can be used as a window onto knowledge, as a word processor, and as an aid to thinking, for example in structuring a topic. In our educational system, there are still too few professors, teachers and mentors who show our young people this approach to the computer.

For critical observers, there is no doubt that the rapid development towards the information and knowledge society challenges businesses to an extent which has never before been experienced, mainly because the businesses themselves, their managers and their staff have not completed, or not been able to complete, the necessary change in thinking. The reason for this is that they do not consider themselves able to match the pace at which IT is changing and expanding the corporate room for manoeuvre. The speed of acceptance and active exploitation by management of new technologies, and the new dimensions of global entrepreneurship which they bring about, is proving to be a critical success factor for businesses of all sizes and in all sectors.

Being prepared for the I-World requires more than the confident handling of the computer and its derived products as tools, as these currently come into being through the merging of information technologies and telecommunications and lead to new forms of mobile commu-

nications, starting with e-mail and progressing through inquiring about stock market levels and concluding trades in Frankfurt, New York or Tokyo in a matter of seconds, to Intranet and Internet transactions. Above all, it demands a different, more flexible thinking, a different way of handling knowledge, an ability to access knowledge rapidly, an ability to find analogies in order to be able to see parallels quickly.

All Change Begins With and Is Effected by the Individual

In the past, and even into modern times, there has been an emphasis on the assimilation and understanding of knowledge. By knowledge, I am referring not just to information which relates to knowledge – but in particular those individual elements of information which have already been processed further. However, the focus of understanding will change. In future, breadth of knowledge will be produced mainly from the ability to handle stored information, by being able to connect blocks of knowledge from areas which appear to have no connection with one another and bringing them into a stimulating new relationship suggestive of new solutions. Creativity hereby gains an added dimension, arising directly from the associative abilities of human thought. Only in a few areas will people still be required to attempt to assimilate and understand specific knowledge down to the last detail. This change from analytical understanding to the application of knowledge will lead to a more rapid increase in available knowledge. In other words, we are developing into a society of users of knowledge, knowledge 'brokers' and knowledge processors. And there is good reason to talk of a new society, one which will also define the new rules for economic activity and economic management.

1.3 The New Technologies: Drivers of Progress

Microelectronics, optoelectronics, micromechanics, gene technology – these new technologies are powerful drivers of progress and economic growth; they are the engines of a change which is affecting practically every area of our lives. The developments in information and telecom-

munications technologies, based on the epoch-defining discoveries and innovations in microelectronics and optoelectronics from the end of the 1950s onwards, have created the decisive preconditions for the way forward into the global real-time information and knowledge society, shaping the path along which we are currently preparing to advance. It is these technologies in particular which make the everyday global division of labour possible, thereby establishing a fundamental precondition for the information society. These technologies minimise or do away with the significance of physical distances, and the time factor. For example, using these technologies, it is possible to make available the critical mass of experts working simultaneously on certain problems, almost immediately and regardless of where they are physically situated. It is only as this electronic networking of the world begins to take shape, or has already come into being within and between the leading industrialised nations, that one can actually talk of globalisation, in the sense of economic structures, on the basis of technological feasibility.

The point in time marking the start of the development of electronics, which has since been pursued with breathtaking speed, can be defined precisely: in 1959, a little over 40 years ago, the American Jack Kilby integrated several transistor functions on a silicon crystal for the first time. This first integrated circuit came at the start of a process of evolution with unforeseeable dimensions and effects – comparable only to the major fundamental innovations of industrial history: the steam engine, the railway, the automobile, plastics. Common to all these fundamental innovations is the fact that they launched massive waves of productivity and thus gave impetus to economic growth and high levels of economic activity. The 'electronic revolution' was favoured by an extremely rapid process of innovation which led, only three years later, to the production of the first digital circuits and the development of simple analogue circuits. Four general trends, which notably are developing continuously and interdependently, have determined the subsequent development of microelectronics: first, chips are getting ever smaller; second, they are simultaneously becoming more complex; third, they are becoming ever faster; and fourth – and of great significance to the breadth of their applications – they are becoming ever cheaper, with a cost reduction potential over a decade which is close on a factor of 100.

Two cycles determine the pace of growth and cost reductions in the microelectronic components industry, thus presenting top management within these companies with complex technological and commercial challenges:

1. The cycle of technological progress, thanks to the core ability of the sector to achieve ever finer strip conductor structures at the sub-micron level, thus being able to integrate ever more storage and/or logic functions on a single chip. Finer structures simultaneously mean shorter operation times for the circuit switches, leading to higher switching speeds and therefore faster processors, storage media, computers, exchanges, robots, engine management systems, navigations systems.

2. The market cycles, which with their marked surges and weak periods in demand subject the capacities of the chip factories and the achievable price level to fluctuations which are just as strong as those experienced in the profit expectations of the processor industry. Despite its markedly cyclical character, this industry remains a growth sector with strong demand for capital.

Each chip generation requires significantly higher investment than its predecessor. Even very large companies enter into strategic alliances in this area, to share out the risks, to exchange process expertise, to handle the growing volumes of investment and to optimise the use of production capacities, which effectively increase automatically with every reduction in the initially high proportion of rejected parts manufactured. The telecommunications industry, the computer industry, the manufacturers of electronic games, and increasingly the automotive industry are the major buyers from the chip industry, which has accrued significant hardware volumes with the transformation in the Internet to become a mass communications medium, and because of the rapid growth in the area of multimedia. Digitisation has led to great surges in demand in gaming electronics – starting with the CD and through to DVD and MD – and in telecommunications (mobile phones, ISDN, DSL), and thus also in microelectronics, and to repeated new challenges for the chip producers. The succession of generations of electronic gaming devices and in the computer and

telecommunications industry largely derives from the rapid succession of generations in the microelectronic components.

With the accelerated advance of digital electronics, the aviation and space industry and above all the companies in the automotive industry with their mass demand have become significant buyers from the chip industry. The former Head of Development at VW, Professor Fiala, indicated as early as the 1980s that almost every advance in the building of automobiles would be delivered by microelectronics. When one thinks of electronic fuel injection (which has replaced a highly complicated mechanical system), engine management, ABS, electronic stability control, anti-block and anti-skid regulators or navigation systems, then one has impressive confirmation of Fiala's prophetic vision.

Fascinating new products and systems have developed out of the interplay between new technologies. Here, for example, one thinks of the whole area of optoelectronics, of the storage media which have developed from this for music, data and moving images (CD, CD-ROM, DVD), of the role of fibreoptic cables as high-capacity broadband transmission channels, which for the first time have enabled the high transmission speeds required by TV and HDTV, and also by the large data flows required by industry. In implementing what was technically possible in new applications, starting with the introduction of TV and colour TV, the classic chicken-and-egg scenario has repeatedly arisen. On the one hand, there is an issue regarding achieving critical mass for the infrastructure and the end devices, while on the other hand there is an issue regarding the breadth of the offer and the quality of content and services (for example telematics). To achieve one, the other is necessary. This often requires significant preparatory work, which as well as needing imagination on the part of the engineers and the salespeople, also requires the providers to take a long-term view. Many other aspects of technological development could be cited at this point to confirm this thesis about the function of modern technologies, which as they are implemented open up new and sizable markets, and with them growth and employment, but space precludes this.

Mention has already been made of the impetus given to growth and the level of economic activity which major fundamental innovations generate. This impetus can only be shared by those economies which also possess segments of the microelectronics, information and telecom-

munications industry which are high-performing and able to compete. The position which Germany and Europe are minded to adopt, or in reality, will be able to adopt, in the future new global knowledge society will be determined to some degree by the development of these industries. Anyone who is dependent on imports of technology from the USA and the Far East cannot keep pace with the global competition. If, in most sectors, the European ICT (information/communications and technology) industry is lagging behind its competitors in the USA and, in some instances, those in Asia, this is in part dependent upon the legislative and regulatory framework conditions for economic activity in Germany and in Europe as a whole, and in part dependent on their inability to exploit fully the technological, creative and innovative abilities and potential of the companies which have established there.

Education and Training – A Decisive Factor for Competing in the I-World

The government of the Netherlands made intelligent use of its accession to the Presidency of the EU Council in 1997 when it made this issue the object of an impressive initiative for a new European policy on research and training. The basis of this was a study,[7] in which Booz Allen Hamilton compiled the results of worldwide benchmarking of the relevant technological and industrial trends and indicators. The central question addressed by the study was: how competitive is Europe, when compared with the USA, Japan and Korea, and what needs to happen at the European policy level to make good deficits in the complex area of the ICT sectors and at all costs not to allow such deficits to become even greater?

The key findings from this study can be summarised in a statement which gives little comfort: overall, the European ICT industry is falling behind its competitors in the USA and, in some instances, those in Asia, in most sectors. In particular, the results of the sectoral analysis give the impression that the Europeans have either stood still or been held back at the midway point in many areas. On the one hand, the share of the European industry in the market for traditional ICT mass products is stagnating, while on the other European providers are falling way

behind their North American competitors in critical growth areas (critical because they are vital for success) such as software development and software applications and content/media. The phenomenal development in the Internet economy has certainly not caused the deficit, identified as early as 1997, to be reduced at all.

Another finding from the study, and one which is not particularly surprising, although it is no less critical in its impact, is the fact that the strongly differing policies towards ICT in the individual countries of the EU – together with different degrees of implementation – have resulted in a highly fragmented European information and telecommunications landscape. As a result, the ability to act on large markets under standardised conditions has been, if not prevented, then at least impaired and delayed. Among the dire consequences of this are the missed opportunities for new jobs, such as have been created in the USA in their millions in these industries. Findings such as these are not without a tragic element, since they describe a twin dilemma. Not only does Europe not have the jobs, unlike those generated in the USA in large numbers, but as the Net economy also creates new employment opportunities in Germany and Europe, there are insufficient well-trained IT experts to fulfill the new tasks. A failed policy on education and training is wreaking its revenge. With great political enthusiasm, there has been discussion of the so-called Green Card. At the same time, it is only too apparent that it will take some time before Europe's academic secondary schools produce school-leavers with excellent knowledge in mathematics, physics and computing in sufficient numbers to satisfy the increasing demands of the economy.

New technologies are proving not only to be drivers of progress, but also engines of affluence in the knowledge society. In the interim, Europe has made a number of important changes in direction. Deregulation is advancing in telecommunications, the energy sector and possibly soon in water supply and distribution across mainland Europe, providing greater competition.

In the area of telecommunications, and specifically in mobile communications, the new technologies offer Europe new opportunities to participate at the very forefront of the future development, on the basis of common standards – the keyword here is UMTS (Universal Mobile Telecommunications System). In this area, there can be no doubt that it

is helpful that alongside Motorola, the other leading global manufacturers of mobile telephone infrastructure equipment and end-user
devices, Siemens, Ericsson and Nokia are European. With UMTS, the
European Telecommunications Standards Institute has set out the technological parameters for a new transmission technology which will offer
mobile telephones access to the Internet and at the same time expands
the Internet by enabling it to be used in a mobile environment as well.
The 3G (third generation) networks and mobile telephones will transmit
speech, video and text information. The development is already far
advanced. While Europe's governments never tire of vaunting their
support for new technologies and progressive infrastructures, the diktat
of budget deficits and empty coffers nevertheless has led to a position
where UMTS licences were auctioned at high prices. This restricts the
number of providers from the outset and leads, of necessity, to oligop-
olies. Providers were compelled to take on high risks and depressing
burdens of debt, which went beyond their investments in the new technology. The logic of support for technology and infrastructure clearly
has its limits when it comes to deficits in the national budget.

The new standard represents a significant modernisation of the
existing cellular network, and it offers high efficiency levels for wireless connections and improved transmission and relaying abilities based
on ATM and IP, thanks to its use of CDMA technology. The high degree
of compatibility of these technologies will in future also support inter-
continental roaming. Expanding the Internet by adding the element of
mobility offers the user definite advantages. Thanks to its higher transmission speed, the new standard permits data communication (for
example for e-mails) and access to the World Wide Web, with the result
that mobile phone operators can offer speech communications at low
prices and compete head to head with the fixed network operators.

The popularity of the Internet has significantly changed the expectations regarding the use of the UMTS networks, and is accelerating their
introduction. The development of telecommunications is increasingly
data-driven today. The higher speed by comparison with previous ISDN
connections is also of similar importance for all those private users who
want to surf the Internet as entertainment, or order a pizza or concert
tickets. It is clear that the multimedia capability of the mobile telephone
will lead to new, combined functionalities and devices. The mobile

phone and the pocket notebook will in future be brought together in the multimedia mobile phone. As the forerunner to UMTS, so to speak, WAP – Wireless Application Protocol – is an interesting, even though so far not successful, example of the speed with which progressive mobile telephone technologies conquer the market, change the type of devices being offered, and extend the potential uses. WAP-enabled mobile phones are equipped with a special microprocessor, making it possible to surf the Internet before the introduction of the universal mobile telephone standard, even if limited mainly to working with text-based Internet content. A dedicated language (WML – Wireless Markup Language) was created for WAP, paring down content for display via the mobile phone. Images, sound files and videos are filtered out by WAP. Such filtered Internet content is available rapidly on the display screen of the WAP-enabled mobile phone.

Complex Corporate Decisions under Extreme Time Pressure

The developments sketched out here, which require corporate decisions in very short time-frames, also represent enormous challenges for top management. Currently, that management is reacting to the radically changed competitive situation in the telecommunications market with a wave of joint ventures, mergers and company purchases costing billions of marks, and also by attempting to increase customer orientation. In these actions, we are also seeing concrete examples of developments being driven by technology and the market, on a scale which has not previously been experienced. In managing the complex effects of this rapid succession of changes on the people and markets involved, exceptional demands are being made of people. What is needed is the ability to convert technological options into market successes, in a climate of ever shorter life-cycles for products and systems in competitive markets where there is almost total transparency. The opportunities for employees to develop their own careers – particularly in the field of technology – are that much better where the employee him- or herself takes a greater responsibility for keeping knowledge up to date, in a process of life-long learning. It is the foremost task of management to provide employees with the encouragement, the incentive and the practical help to do so.

1.4 The Competitive Economy: Maturity Not Monopoly

The paradox of deregulation to define the market is evident: an intervention by the state, a politically motivated act of state on the part of the legislature, is required to set free those energies to improve efficiency and customer orientation, through liberalisation which creates competition for the first time or significantly intensifies that competition. As early as 1978, this was the decisive impetus behind the deregulation of air travel in the USA, and following that for the privatisation of major formerly nationalised companies such as British Petroleum, British Aerospace, British Telecom and British Airways in the Thatcher era in Great Britain, and of course for the much later corresponding deregulation projects in Germany as well. Competition leads on the one hand to price reductions and innovations. On the other hand, it provides impulses for the development of the market, with corresponding scale effects which make it possible for well-managed companies to realise higher profits even in a situation of falling margins. For top management, this powerful stimulus for growing productivity and increased competitive ability resulted in a sustained drive to restructure businesses – a drive whose effects can be studied from numerous examples, not least by looking at the ex-monopoly company Deutsche Telekom AG. Ultimately, in liberal competitive markets significantly more jobs are created with the new, alternative providers than may possibly be lost by the ex-monopoly provider. Thus there is a notable component which impacts on people even in the apparently unpromising issue of deregulation.

In the telecommunications sector, the moves towards deregulation began relatively late in Germany, by comparison with other countries. However, the competition – once liberated from the old restrictions and ultimately licensed very rapidly and smoothly – then entered the contest with some enthusiasm. It offered the consumer significantly lower telecommunications costs, but at the same time a barely comprehensible jungle of tariffs as the typical outcome of the drive to differentiation under which the market participants were striving to improve their chances in the market. Since then, the first mergers/sales have been completed of German businesses in this sector, as expected (Otelo to Mannesmann Arcor, E-Plus from RWE and VEBA to France Telecom), reflecting increasing competitive pressure with consequent falling

margins in the face of high start-up losses. The announcement of an unfriendly takeover bid for Mannesmann by Vodafone Airtouch had the media and shareholders in suspense for several months, and provoked extraordinary swings in stock markets and moods. The managements of both businesses initiated a spectacular flurry of activities and creativity which was watched with astonishment by the general public. Remarkably, the issue of the correlations between an unfriendly takeover and the integration of corporate cultures played no significant part in the discussions. Further buy-outs and mergers, particularly among the smaller providers, have either already been realised, as evidenced by the purchasing activities of MobilCom CEO Schmid, the participation by France Telecom in MobilCom, the purchase of Orange, similarly by France Telecom, or the acquisition of E-Plus by KPN, or continue to be announced – hastened not least by huge, fantasy-provoking mergers like that between AOL and Time-Warner. Since the bubble of speculation burst, little of this euphoria has lasted. Even the well-filled Deutsche Telekom 'war chest' will in the long term not merely serve to provoke speculation, but will be deployed in a targeted fashion for the necessary process of internationalisation (VoiceStream).

Before Privatisation of Water Supply and Distribution

In the energy sector within Germany, deregulation has only just begun. The first effects, in the sense of greater competition, are now apparent in the form of falling electricity prices. On the other hand, we are also seeing the announcement of major company mergers (following the merger of Badenwerk and Energieversorgung Schwaben to form EnBW, at the end of September 1999 came the announcement of the now-completed mergers of VEBA and VIAG in the new E.ON or RWE and VEW) that force the intensified competition to embrace new orders of size. This trend will not only be a lasting one, but it is likely to increase at the global level, as has recently been demonstrated by the participation of the French energy group EdF in EnBW. E.ON had barely become established as a new name in the energy sector before the idea for even bigger, trans-border co-operations was raised, which may ultimately lead to a new merger. Further significant potential for greater competition

through deregulation, and thus for desirable economic effects, lies in the areas of banking (even if occasionally this potential may fail to be realised) and insurance, in the large and economically significant transportation branch (with the example being the takeovers of Danzas and DHL by Deutsche Post AG), and also in the public sector, but above all in the area of water supply and distribution, which is still a protected geographically based monopoly. The very number of water supply and distribution companies currently operating in Germany – 9000 – demonstrates that in this area we are dealing with what might euphemistically be termed a very 'tradition-rich' structure. In principle, however, the conditions applicable to this sector are comparable to those of the energy sector: production, transmission, distribution, marketing and sales do not need to remain permanently in the hands of a local or at best a regional monopoly – even if to date, unlike energy supply, there is no connecting water system for large geographical areas. In terms of the technology, however, this does not present any problems, as is evidenced by the large conurbations on the Rhine and the Ruhr, the water supply to major cities such as Stuttgart, or the large French water company groups, including Vivendi (as the tradition-rich Compagnie Générale des Eaux is known today) which is among the biggest players in the market for water services. Its marketing skills, incidentally, were a key to entry into the telecommunications market, in a joint venture with British Telecom and Cegetel. In its next move, Vivendi sought to link up with the TV and film activities of Seagrams, showing an understanding of the ever-increasing importance of content.

Vivendi's original area of activities comprises a market with huge volume, which until now has been shielded from any competition. At the same time, in dealing with water one is dealing with a resource which, in global terms, is scarce and becoming ever more scarce as the world population increases – a resource over which disputes and struggles are already being waged today, with the likelihood that this will increase in future. In the German water supply and distribution sector, there is a growing opinion that the process of deregulation will be unstoppable in this area too. Ortwin Scholz, President of the European Union of National Associations of Water Suppliers and Waste Water Services (Eureau) and member of the board for the Berlin water supply and distribution company Berliner Wasserbetriebe, stated this very

clearly at an international conference in Berlin in autumn 1999. He said that the German water supply and distribution sector was faced with an unprecedented wave of consolidation within the industry. He noted that in Great Britain the process was already underway and very wide-ranging. Of the original 3500 suppliers, only 10 regional and 14 local companies remained. In the Netherlands too, privatisation of the water supply and distribution industry is already well advanced – and there too, it was associated with a wave of consolidations.

Demands on the Authorities: Treat Citizens as Customers

When it comes to the authorities, deregulation should be aimed particularly at making life easier for citizens in their dealings with the authorities. In the age of the Internet and the Intranet, I consider it an unacceptable anachronism that in Germany, for example, a citizen can only renew his or her passport in the place where they live, even though the exchange of data required between the authorities would take a matter of seconds; nor can electronic signature be considered a problem any longer, since the law on signatures came into force in 1997. However, even in this area there are the first signs of attempts at a more citizen-friendly approach through the decentralisation and removal of bureaucracy from the functions of the authorities. In 1998, the German federal government issued a nationwide competition for civic bodies called Media@Kom, with the aim of encouraging the use of the electronic signature. The victors were the cities of Nuremberg and Esslingen and the State of Bremen, for their respective concepts. In Bremen, the work to develop One Stop Government has progressed a considerable way. In its system, all administrative systems are to be bundled together, irrespective of whether they are provided by the local commune, the state or federal government. The system is to include free operators and service providers operating in the private sector. Security is an important aspect of this – and a critical precondition for broad acceptance. The citizen will receive a smart card which can also be used to carry out financial transactions – in other words, a comprehensive system of e-Government. Approaches to e-Government are discussed in greater detail in section 2.5. Here, we are mainly dealing with the aspect of deregulation.

Berlin launched an initiative to encourage multimedia projects, called
'Project future'. An expansion of the city information system is on the
agenda, as is expanding the possibilities of interactive administration. To
date, around 7000 documents on all aspects of life in the city have already
been made available for calling up, including, for example, forms for the
notification of taking up or leaving residence for the registration authorities (a legal requirement in Germany when moving to a new place of
residence). In future, the citizen should be able to avoid many wearisome
processes involving the authorities by performing the tasks from his or
her home. In the area of education and training, Berlin's 'Project future'
should mean that all schools in the city-state of Berlin are equipped with
PCs and an Internet connection. A critic might observe that this is
happening rather late in the day, but we must not forget that the larger part
of the city was only reunited with West Berlin a decade ago.

1.5 Knowledge: From a Power Lever to a Production Lever

The development towards a knowledge society which we are experiencing now is generating change far beyond the level of businesses, in
society and in the world we live in; these are lasting changes, although
today we have only the broad outlines of such changes, and they occur at
a speed of which many people are not aware, or rather of which they will
become aware only very late on. As always, this development probably
first begins with the young, even with the very young. For them, the
Internet today is as much a part of the fabric of their lives as the television
or the video recorder was 25 or 30 years ago, when they became a regular
part of everyday household goods. Culture and attitudes to life change in
tandem with these changes in the world, and mostly – much to the chagrin
of all the harbingers of doom among the intelligentsia, predicting the
demise of culture – in an overwhelmingly positive direction.

If the information society was and is mainly characterised by the
recording, storing and distributing of knowledge, then the knowledge
society advances to the next level of processing and applying knowledge – in a process resembling cell division in nature, so to speak.
Knowledge is the only natural raw material which is not consumed, but
rather increased, through use. For a long time, and even today, infor-

mation technology has lacked the element of creative association of ideas, that process of associative thinking which makes the human brain such an amazing thing. High-performance Internet search engines are the first approaches towards realising similar abilities to make associations, even if currently they are mainly limited to help functions, such as the rapid retrieval of information, providing a quick overview of large amounts of information, and fast access to selected information, which is then converted into knowledge by human beings. Nevertheless, search engines are already indicating possible bridges between different components of knowledge. That is a very important step forward.

Originally land, labour and capital defined the critical levers for production, forming the magic triangle of the economy. In the interim, knowledge – albeit remarkably late in the day – has been identified as the fourth major lever influencing production, and has become an economic lever of truly dramatic importance. 'The assets of a company always also include the sum of what its employees are capable of', is how Dr Leopold K. Fara of the Paderborn Institute for Applied Economic Psychology expresses this phenomenon,[8] thereby identifying the significant potential for adding value which lies in the knowledge held by employees. Today, there is no longer any doubt regarding the status of knowledge as a critical lever for competition and success within the corporate context. Capital is engaged in a focused search for the best knowledge, and to that end invests in venture companies whose prospects for growth result from the knowledge focused in intelligent business start-ups. Capital is on the lookout for knowledge, innovation, creativity. Knowledge is mobile, and effortlessly leaps the boundaries passed down over time. It is thought-provoking that only a little over five per cent of global knowledge is produced in Germany nowadays, according to a statement by Professor Dr Meyer-Krahmer.[9] It is only in those places where knowledge is created and converted at an early stage into innovations that prosperity develops, and new jobs can be created. Decisively influenced in earlier times by geography (water power, waterways, rail connections), the presence of mineral resources (wood, coal, ore) and the availability of labour, the importance of location today is not as high as it was formerly. In the knowledge society, spatial and intellectual isolationism have been made practically impossible. Countries, regions and cities can instead gain competitive advantages today

by targeted encouragement and development of the production lever of knowledge. This generates the power to attract capital and people.

Knowledge Creates the Power to Innovate, and Generates Employment

In those countries where people are not sufficiently open to other ideas and energies are not focused consistently on knowledge and innovation, unemployment remains a burning issue (and to a considerable extent, for precisely these reasons). The universities, the state and private initiatives have reacted faster in the USA than elsewhere to the new demands of the knowledge-based economy and, as a result, many more new jobs have been created there than in the German-speaking region. This is because of the greater innovation and creativity that is released, and also because there is a readiness to provide services, which continue to be underdeveloped in Germany. In addition, the link between education and training policy, the power to innovate and employment is becoming apparent. The sober term 'employment' hardly allows the human dimension of the issue to come through; it masks the ethical challenge which lies in creating satisfying tasks for people in the new world of work.

It is undeniably the case that knowledge resides first and foremost in the individual person – and above all in the individual's ability to process knowledge, to associate knowledge and to apply that knowledge to good effect; this remains true irrespective of all the sophisticated information systems, with their immense storage capacity and their ever faster possibilities for accessing information. It therefore seems reasonable to see a connection between the 'discovery' of knowledge (perhaps it is simply a matter of developing an awareness?) and the renaissance of human resources.

Renaissance of Human Resources Deriving from the Greater Functionality of the Human Brain

In moving towards the knowledge society, the function of the human brain attains, so to speak, a different and, to put it optimistically, a higher

level. The academic and journalist Gertrud Höhler[10] has considered the psychological and philosophical background to this phenomenon:

> The separation between machine-processed knowledge and human experience will become ever clearer. The self-awareness of the individual by comparison with his 'intelligent' machine will increase rather than decrease in the course of this separation: for the first time, the human brain will have the opportunity to delegate all mechanical, complex and multi-part work processes to computers. The individual's mental capacity will thus be freed up for tasks which the computer cannot imitate: these are the processing of knowledge into reserves of experience, and working creatively with knowledge and experience to renew culture.

Höhler draws the following conclusion:

> The triumphant march of the computer, which relieves us of the burden of mundane thought processes, is associated with the triumphant march of human distinctiveness and originality.

The remarkable thing about these sentences is above all that they were written 15 years ago. They describe a future which in the meantime has long since become a reality.

For simple storage of information, the human brain today makes use of IT largely as a matter of course; the brain can then concentrate more on the association and application of elements of knowledge. Professor Dr Hans-Jürgen Warnecke, President of the Fraunhofer Gesellschaft, a research support body, sees in this a paradigm shift which is having an impact on academic work:

> Because new things mostly develop at the interfaces with other disciplines, the marked specialisation which has developed in the academic world is becoming a restriction. In future, the specialist must become able to communicate to a considerable degree beyond that specialism, in order to collaborate in changing interdisciplinary teams.[11]

This statement can be transferred in full and applied to innovation processes in economic enterprises:

In a similar manner, industry is freeing itself from the old model of Taylorism, the perfectly organised division of labour. In place of rigid divisions and rigid hierarchical structures, we have teamwork, flat hierarchies and flexible structures. The new paradigms are guided by the organisational structures in nature: fractals, independent units associating themselves into networks through self-organisation.[11]

Where this interdisciplinary association is successful, where the human ability to engage in associative thinking can unfold in full (something which the computer can currently still only achieve at a rudimentary level, as I have already remarked), new knowledge is generated in a creative process, and through it new skills. The individual is developing into a rapid and productive 'knowledge generator'. At the same time, this implies the no doubt difficult and in no way automatic departure from the inherited role of the individual as knowledge-carrier, someone who considers that knowledge as his or her own personal lever for power and success and who is therefore not prepared to share knowledge. We must be under no illusions that in this area we are being asked to overcome the barriers of instinctive human behaviour. Guided by a deeply rooted sense of self and an instinct for self-preservation, every one of us has a tendency to be unwilling to share any part of his or her knowledge. Ultimately, employees will only divulge their personal knowledge if on the one hand they develop sufficient self-confidence, and on the other hand they have the necessary confidence in the company that it is pursuing the right course – a course which also advances them personally. Knowledge management, addressed in greater detail in section 3.7, also means handling people carefully for that reason, smoothing their path through far-reaching changes in their learned behaviours and encouraging thinking in networks of combinations. Nothing at all can be achieved through a simple directive from above when it comes to realising this change.

If one takes a sober look at the current structures in politics and economics, then in many areas the traditional view still seems to prevail: 'Knowledge is power – the power to arrange and to change things. The knowledge of how to exercise authority serves the purpose of retaining power.' This view is outdated in two regards – first, isolated knowledge is becoming of ever less use to the individual, and second,

the skills of working with knowledge are only generated in a network. On the other hand, sceptical observers also know that the Internet not only presents an ideal medium for the dissemination of knowledge or simply of information, but also a medium which can be used to penetrate the security ring around knowledge of how to exercise authority.

Discussions with top managers have demonstrated to me that there is no consensus on these issues. The opposite conviction is also expressed, that knowledge of how to exercise authority is becoming of greater importance, even in – indeed, especially in – the age of the Internet. The argument behind this is that the identification and definition of essential changes, through the creative association of complex facts and assumptions about the future, takes place in the heads of a few top managers, or (to spell it out more fully) in the heads of the élite of top performers.

Open Questions About Knowledge as a Power Lever

Beyond the open questions about knowledge as a power lever, it has become apparent that managing knowledge has a lot to do with the ability to change patterns of human behaviour. Whether the knowledge society of the 21st century will be a more humane society or will give added impetus to the isolation of the individual, which leads in turn to the autism of the one-dimensional hackers and Internet freaks, depends critically on how people handle their new opportunities, on how they come to terms with and exploit the new pace of change. For our educational system, this opens up wholly new perspectives and challenges. The principle of life-long learning becomes an indispensable element in securing one's livelihood in the knowledge society.

This much is clear to all those who have an understanding of these matters: even in the knowledge society, there will still be many people who are intellectually unable to pursue the required level of knowledge and who are incapable of working out and applying that degree of understanding for themselves. For these people, a world which is increasingly defined by knowledge will be barely more humane than the old world of work, which at least provided them with wages and food. The Nuremberg Institute for Employment Market and Career Research, in a study conducted jointly with Prognos AG, Basle, came to the

conclusion that just over 1.5 million unskilled jobs will be lost in Germany by 2010. Many of these people have skills which are not those of knowledge workers. There is an element of tragedy in the fact that these skills are no longer needed, or are needed only to a limited extent. According to this study, the proportion of unskilled work in the total employment market will shrink from 19 to 16 per cent. The novelist and semiotics expert Umberto Eco, famous worldwide for his novel *The Name of the Rose,* spoke recently at the world economic forum in Davos of a new three-class society, in which the members of the lowest class, the proletariat, 'can only watch television and pre-formed images', while Eco believes that the members of the middle class, the 'bourgeoisie', will at least still be able to use the computer to take out money or to buy something. Businesses and society are responsible for bringing on these people through their training and continuous training programmes so that they understand and can make use of simpler areas of knowledge.

The issue of education offers wide scope for private and corporate initiatives, far beyond the efforts being made by the state which are still inadequate. In this area, there are increasingly encouraging developments. Hasso Plattner, the co-founder and CEO of SAP, established a model programme in 1999 which merits being called exemplary, because it shows how a future-oriented training requirement generated by the demands of the modern software industry is recognised and satisfied by a far-sighted employer in precisely that industry. Over the coming 20 years, he is to commit a total of DM100 million from his personal assets, with the money being donated for academic training at the Hasso Plattner Institute for Software Systems Engineering at Potsdam University. In October 1999, the first graduate students enrolled on this seven-semester course in software systems engineering. Plattner's example has already served as a catalyst for other initiatives.

1.6 Social Change: The Self-aware Generation

As the new century begins, economic enterprises are operating in the context of a society which Neil Postman[12] observed 15 years earlier was amusing itself to death – long before the Internet mutated from the

knowledge network into the biggest entertainment machine in the world, which is certainly among its qualities in addition to all its practical functions. If one holds that there is a certain correlation between amusement and consumption, then Postman's assertion can also be viewed as an originally expressed and media-focused description of that far-reaching social change which Jürgen Habermas defined in his work *The Structural Change of the Public Sphere* nearly 40 years earlier as a change from the reasoning to the consuming society.[50]

Peter Glotz, a long-time pioneer and lateral thinker for German social democracy, has said that we are living in a society where 'the sense of sympathy with the common good has been used up by the Nazis, and later by the Communists'.[13] Whether the Stalinists, the Nazis or the Communists were the initiators of this 'consumption' of what was formerly a valuable quality remains an unanswered question. To my mind, it is a serious enough matter that not only can one justify the analysis that the common good is no longer a serviceable and ideal concept, but the very phrase itself is often presented as something from a previous era, to be cast aside in distrust. To that, one can add that service and fulfilling one's obligations are no longer values which can automatically be taken for granted.

Today's society increasingly lacks a binding canon of values. In a corporate context, shared ideas about values, and the behaviour patterns guided by these ideas, are therefore imbued with even greater importance. In the knowledge and service society, with its increasingly strongly project-based commitment of employees, this holds true to an even greater extent than for the old-style industrial society which was hierarchically managed.

The perception of social responsibility in a conflict-laden and frequently also conflict-ready environment presupposes above all social competence, alongside the lived common values; this competence is sometimes termed emotional intelligence – one of the essential characteristics and abilities of successful management figures of the present and the future. Managing complex change processes successfully, and in particular those processes which are continually taking place and which in every instance affect people, is only possible if one possesses precisely this social competence, which is considered in greater detail in section 3.2.

A further notable, significant and positive change in society during the 1990s was the new, self-aware sense of the role of women, and the newly defined position of women in society, in politics, and in the economy. It is no more a matter of chance that today a woman heads up a global business like Hewlett Packard, than is the fact that skilled women such as Hertha Däubler-Gmelin and Jutta Limbach hold the highest offices in the German judiciary; to say nothing of the former US American Secretary of State, Madeleine Albright and the present security advisor, Condoleeza Rice. The successful woman has taken her rightful place among the new élite of top performers. Equality of opportunity is on the increase, even if there is still some way to go.

Value Orientation and Elites are Indispensable

In post-war Germany, however, over four decades the opinion that élites are indispensable was steadfastly (or would it be more honest to say 'narrow-mindedly'?) denied: even a society undergoing radical change needs élites, and furthermore it needs élites which merit the term value-stable. The turbulent upheavals in the German political landscape have more than clearly demonstrated where things can lead if this strict value orientation is lost. 'The progress of culture in complex societies depends, as in the past, on the activities of fairly small minorities', is how this view is expressed by Peter Glotz, Rita Süssmuth and Konrad Seitz in their book *The Planless Elites*.[13] Major, internationally active businesses are in some aspects very similar to these 'complex societies'.

'I am telling you about a country where mediocrity has become the ruling and dominant force. The word "elite" has become a derogatory term.' These are the words of the Deputy President of the Central Committee of Jews in Germany and CDU politician Michel Friedman, who is very committed to European policy, as he passed harsh judgement on the social and political reality in Germany at the Booz Allen Hamilton Employers' Forum 2000: 'We find ourselves in a society where responsibility is not a lived experience.' He argued that our sense of self-understanding and our perception of reality are damaged and limited. He summarised this by saying: 'In Germany, we don't make enough effort' and 'If we take responsibility seriously, then we cannot go on like this.'

However, Friedman does not just issue warnings, but is also a cautious optimist: 'Never before has Europe had such a real opportunity for peace and freedom as today.' But he is also aware that 'it depends on us, on our generation'. Friedman sees the entrepreneur as having direct social and political responsibility: 'There is no bell-tower, no microcosmic world of corporate action.' For Friedman, the decisive issue is 'that we again make the effort to talk with one another and to grapple with one another'. He emphasises his understanding of the culture of conflict: 'It is a false understanding which people have when they think that they must be liked by everyone else.'

Companies must react to this rapid social change – there is no dissent on that point. Their social responsibility, and thus that of management, is unalterable and cannot be delegated. On the other hand, individual businesses, and even new technologies, can not only react to social and economic change, but they can also initiate, accelerate or put the brake on such change. One only has to think of fundamental inventions like the transistor, the integrated circuit, the computer or optoelectronics. Names like Johannes Gutenberg, Gottlieb Daimler, Henry Ford, Werner von Siemens, Carl Zeiss or – to jump to the present day – Bill Gates illuminate and make clear the role of the innovators, inventors, entrepreneurs and businesses as engines of social change in our era. The interdependence of society and culture, economy and technologies is increasingly in evidence.

At the same time, the mobility of the individual is a form of link which is becoming ever more important. Great Britain and the Netherlands are classic examples of the status of personal mobility and flexibility in countries and societies whose economies grew up with colonial traditions, and where the home market was always too restricting for the expansionist ambitions of their economies. In these countries, an international career in management – with the acceptance of the burdens this imposed on family, everyday living conditions and health – was simply a matter of fact from the early days of the trading companies and industrialisation, while, in contrast, it was unusual and almost exceptional, in Germany up until the mid-20th century. The readiness to embrace mobility has shaped the societies in these countries in a lasting fashion – right through to their clubs and the songs which they particularly love and sing together.

Naturally, mobility is not without its dangers, and naturally flexibility loosens ties. The critical counterweight to this is the family unit, which because of increasing life expectancy can be seen in growing measure as a three-generation family. In a notable essay, Professor Norbert Walter, chief economist for Deutsche Bank, writes:

> The family is irreplaceable as an economic community binding destinies and loyalties together, if only for the simple reason that the collectivities of the state, despite all the attempts made with the full extent of its energies, cannot provide the services delivered by the family in a manner which either does justice to human feelings or which is economically efficient – as is demonstrated by the past 25 years of European socialism. While the role of the family as a unit with a shared economic destiny can be called into question, at least at the level of theory, the family is absolutely irreplaceable for the provision of happiness and protection as the basis for education and training. It is only where generations, genders and siblings mix together that the ability to live develops, in the elemental and in the spiritual sense.[14]

Social competence, the most undervalued qualification which employees possess, develops precisely and primarily in the seed cell of the family. I can only endorse every word of this important plea for the family, a plea which seeks to conserve the values that it communicates. However, the growing number of single people speaks another, sobering language. Happiness and protection in the single-person household require, by contrast, an unusual power of the imagination. Doubtless these are the phenomena of a society in transition, where Sennett's 'flexible individual' (see Chapter 4) acts with rare uncertainty, because instead of wrestling his way through to achieve flexibility, he is overwhelmed by it. However, here too we find that a development back towards a value-stable group – be it the family, a circle of friends or a business – is becoming increasingly important. The logical conclusion of this development, with regard to corporate priorities, must be an increasing importance attaching to values-based management, as is examined in greater detail in sections 3.2 and 3.4.

CHAPTER 2

The Human Element at the Heart of Entrepreneurial Challenge

2.1 Mastering Change – Developing Flexibility, Making the Transformation

In a globalised economic world, experienced as the forum for competition which spans the world, change is proving to be the only reliable constant. Businesses are living organisms in this world. More than ever before, they need to be ready and able to adapt constantly and flexibly to the changing economic, technological and social context in which they operate. Gertrud Höhler expressed this dramatic change in quite poetic terms: 'The future is seeping into all areas of life and is sowing unrest.'[10] Alongside this dominant element of change comes a second, equally influential – I am tempted to say 'omnipresent' – phenomenon: the extraordinary acceleration and pace of processes. This results in challenges which management can only overcome with a comprehensively well-founded strategic view. If it is accurate to state – and no one is doubting that it is – that change is a permanent process in the life of a business, then to a large extent management is necessarily change management (and only to a limited extent, routine). In other words, change management is not the exception but the rule in the life of a manager at the start of the third millennium.

It is immediately apparent, given the global competition, that no management can now afford not to identify performance reserves within

the business, or to leave these reserves unexploited. On the other hand, numerous discussions with managers from the widest range of businesses worldwide confirm the general experience, of both life and management, that long-term performance improvements are difficult to realise and can only be attained with great effort, which definitely makes them far more difficult to achieve than more fashionable short-term goals. Even businesses with outstanding strategic initiatives and efficient organisational structures are faced with this problem. Existing management systems are often not a suitable tool for satisfactorily achieving the objective of a sustained performance improvement. They often provide only inadequate support in implementing strategic plans at the level of operative decision-making, often because management does not universally view itself as a factor in implementation following successful development of a vision and an architecture – above all because change management is often the active breaking down of existing structures.

Traditional planning, budgeting and internal reporting systems concentrate mainly on financial control ratios or are limited to *ex-post* observations, instead of looking at the factors influencing actual operating decisions, making information available which is relevant to decision-making, and creating that organisational networking which is indispensable for the realisation of sustained performance improvements. Ultimately, that performance improvement can only be produced by individual employees; as in the past, it is the individual who is at the heart of things. Immediately, the next problem arises: decision-makers in a post of responsibility within a line management system react to the lack of links by constructing their own tailored operative control and key ratio systems – however, this is typically established as an island solution, divorced from the control section within the business. There are serious defects in such systems resulting from the lack of a link with the financial ratios used by the control section, and, for example, in the lack of distinction made between controllable factors (which can be influenced) and exogenous factors which cannot be influenced, or can only be influenced indirectly. Above all, however, such systems tell the user nothing about the true performance potential of the unit to be managed, and therefore offer no starting points for measures to improve performance.

The new strategic management paradigm in the 21st century must, however, be directed towards vitalising all functions and business units – and to do so using the leitmotif of more people-focused management, committed to a lasting canon of values. The new strategic alignment can only achieve full effectiveness if it goes hand in hand with a new alignment in thinking, which does not 'use' the individual like some interchangeable tool but respects the individual's worth, helping him or her to develop and perfect abilities, and willingly, indeed enthusiastically, allowing the individual to do so.

Flexibility as a corporate attitude reflects the rapid changes in markets and in the requirements of customers in terms of products and services. It finds its expression in modern forms of decentralised business organisation with flat hierarchies, as presented in this and the two following sections.

Calls for the need to make businesses flexible are heard everywhere in management meetings and at forums and seminars. Everyone appears to understand that achieving this flexibility under conditions of the pace of business imposed and offered by global competition demands different management structures and a different management style. It is almost a necessity that decentralised and more flexible structures require the predominant management style within a company to be one of partnership, based on trust (sometimes referred to as the trusting organisation) and supporting flexibility. Centrally managed partnerships – although this too is a logical consequence of the new alignment towards future-enabled management structures – are nevertheless threatened with extinction. Rigidly organised hierarchical and centralistic structures and flexibility are a contradiction in terms. If someone is always having to check back as to whether he is allowed to do something, then he simply cannot be sufficiently flexible and self-motivated and display the readiness to react and the speed of action which this new world demands. As is already apparent, ultimately this achievable/desirable degree of flexibility in a business derives from the ability and the inner readiness of managers and employees to show trust, and with it increased flexibility.

In globally operating businesses, mobility (even at the lower levels of the hierarchy) is an important element in flexibility – specified in contracts to work abroad (which existed even at a time when no one

was talking about globalisation), and realised in transfers which can be associated with imposed changes in practically every aspect of one's living circumstances. Anyone who is prepared to build up a sales organisation in the Far East or Africa for his or her business will soon discover the kind of life-changing decisions which are bound up with it. Countries with a wealth of experience of economic operations in former colonies have known about these associated problems for generations. The 'new style' foreign manager, as described in the media, is not so new after all. What is new, however, are the communications and information technologies which make his global tasks of co-ordination easier.

A Global Strategy Demands a Local Presence

Despite the Internet and the satellite telephone, a local presence remains as essential as ever, if, when and wherever one is looking to influence or change people's thinking and actions and build up relationships between people – irrespective of whether they are customers, suppliers or one's own employees. The physical and mental demands resulting from the need for mobility can be very high. Not everyone is up to these demands. That is why, even without any ideological blinkers, critical questions remain to be answered: how much flexibility can reasonably be expected of people in a company, assuming that there is a people-focused management style? And how much can they be expected to bear, taking into consideration the core of their personality and their private social ties? It is apparent that, just as there can be no guarantee of a job for life, similarly, today there can be no life-long guarantee of employment in the same location, in the same department, in the same operating environment.

Psychologists, sociologists and other '-ologists' are wont to associate flexibility with the pessimistic view of the future that 'life is uncertain'. In the search for work, they point out, more and more families are moving from town to town. Families break up and are formed anew. Friends move away, new friends come, until there comes a time where you yourself are moving to somewhere new. 'We are divorcing ourselves from location' is how a design specialist refers to this partial move

towards a nomadic existence in the society of the future. 'The "flexible individual" – protagonist of the great erosion of society or the core of a model for mankind for the coming era?' asks Matthias Horx, an eloquent researcher of trends and the manager of the Institute for the Science of the Future, in his essay 'Welcome to the century of the new nomads'[15] – and ultimately his answers to this question are optimistic ones. Naturally, he can see the dark side of this major change: 'We will spend a lot of our time travelling. A new age of the nomad has begun.' Horx provides impressive forecast figures to explain the new mobility, and laments that:

> we are spending our lives in queues, in temporary arrangements, in transitional stages. We are waiting for the call-down order. Jobs have only just started when they stop again, in the constant maelstrom of mergers.

But against this, Horx argues:

> But if we are really to understand the new mobility, we must learn to understand it on a higher level: as the friction heat of the passing of an era from the industrial age and the coming knowledge economy, as a (possible) core Utopia of a new model for mankind.

Phrases like these should not be a cause for rash celebration. And given the experiences of this and the previous generation, I find scepticism towards everything proclaiming a 'new model for mankind' appropriate. A period of sober reflection is called for.

Horx views the new milieu of the self-aware, self-reliant creative individuals of the 'Self plc' as heralds of what is to come; this is the free agent movement which is already endemic in the USA, where what matters is self-organisation rather than hierarchy, independence rather than wage dependency, the work portfolio rather than the career path. This is expressed in fairly dramatic terms. But it is also an expression full of hope and encouragement – encouragement even in the knowledge that this cannot be the way forward for the mass of working people as currently constituted. In their book *The Custom Enterprise.com*,[16] Gaby Wiegran and Hardy Koth show the intelligent opportunities offered by e-Business to react to the progressive personalisation and individualisation of customer requirements – with tailor-made businesses which operate in

each instance with a narrowly focused vision on the single customer, who behaves like a purchasing 'Self plc'. In other words, the producer 'Self plc' is counterpoised to the consumer 'Self plc'.

In the 21st century, the ability to change and adapt rapidly is more than ever before an essential element enabling businesses to survive, and equally a factor in determining the continued economic existence of the individual in the wider economic context. Incidentally, the generation of those who are now 60 or older has had to learn this lesson painfully late in many cases, since they began their careers in times of what today is barely imaginable constancy, with what appeared to be firmly established hierarchical orders and a sense of 'security' which was to prove deceptive. The change in the relationships between businesses and employees is wide-ranging, and demands considerable qualities in terms of leading people and handling responsibility from top management. This key aspect merits separate and detailed treatment. In sections 3.2 and 3.6, this issue is considered in detail. It deserves a high priority on the CEO agenda.

The Ability to Change is Vital for Survival

Every strategically based transformation which goes beyond simply identifying potential savings can only be understood as a permanent process – permanent, like all those changes in politics, economics and society to which businesses have to adapt if they are not to fossilise and go under. For that reason, transformation processes cannot be aimed solely at breaking up older organisational structures in order to replace them with new structures which are similarly rigid. Admittedly these may provide employees with the advantage of a clear order, but at the same time they convey a false impression of that kind of permanence and stability in which one might again 'settle down' confidently. Rather, transformation must have the objective of developing new, flexible organisms which are equipped to facilitate future change without discontinuities and frictions.

Transformation means disturbance in businesses. There are good reasons for viewing this disturbance positively and constructively. 'The bank never stops, and it must never be allowed to stop', is how Rolf-

Ernst Breuer phrased this idea for Deutsche Bank.[53] And he added that no employee should now ask the question about whether an end-point had been reached following the restructuring currently underway. Rather, it should be understood 'that we must always be faster than the change in a rapidly changing world'. As newspapers commented: 'Restructuring as a permanent state of being is therefore to some extent part of the set programme.' Former Schering Financial Manager Klaus Pohle, in a presentation of a new 'power strategy' for the company in November 1999, took the issue a step further: 'The objective is to reinvent a business every ten years. It is not easy, but we will achieve it!'[17] Pohle and his colleagues on the board believe that they are by no means the only people faced with this task. The political classes, too, will have to become familiar with the fact that change is inevitable.

'Conversion from the supertanker to the fleet of speedboats' is the slogan being applied to earnings-weak, lumbering conglomerates. There are models and trailblazers for this slogan and its successful implementation. Major company groups such as ABB, Bertelsmann or even Deutsche Telekom AG are working with greater effort to find the optimal degree of decentralisation which works for them. At ABB, the process has already been taken so far that, following significant decentralisation, important central emphases are now being redefined, for example global processes for standardised alignment to the strategy of the whole company group and the so-called shared services operation for the realisation of synergy potentials and also to improve service quality. Bertelsmann is another internationally admired example of a flexible, decentralised organisation. Today, the media group comprises more than 300 profit centres operating autonomously on the market.

Making Apparent the Individual Opportunity in Change

The far-reaching necessary processes for change which are being considered or which have already been completed in many large companies will only succeed if the readiness to accept change and participate actively in framing that change is evoked and kept alive in the minds of the people involved. To put it another way: change processes in which rational and emotional factors play an equally important role only have

a prospect of lasting success if the people in the company do not shy away in anxiety when faced with those changes which affect themselves and their work and – in an understandable reaction – display overt or, even worse, covert resistance.

Top management which does not merely pay lip service to the people factor by writing it into its management principles must be able to communicate credibly the fact that change also represents a chance for the individual, and includes a deliberately thought-through opportunity for the individual to actively realise his or her own potential. If it is right that the people in a business form the critical success factor in all change processes – and no one doubts this – then it is only logical that the people factor is the decisive component of a person's character and conduct, which top managers use to handle this permanent process of change successfully. This is particularly true since it is vitally important that change must move from the bottom to the top, and vice versa.

In this context, 'active' is an important keyword: where there is success in winning employees as active participants in framing change, rather than putting in place only a few (generally too few) change agents, the prospects for the transformation process are good. Transformation processes are thus to a large extent communication processes. Respect for soft factors plays a key role in the entire process.

It is also apparent that there are no guaranteed standard formulae or single combination of management styles for transformation processes, just as there are none for turnaround situations, given that the starting points vary from company to company. We all know this to be a truism from the earliest classes at business school. Yet the demand for 'the' solution is repeatedly voiced by distressed managers. However, you should be wary of consultants who answer a demand such as this with a self-confident 'I have the solution'. This incessant desire for ever new management methods and concepts is reflected in a diligent collection of 300 such concepts into a book entitled *The A–Z of Management Practice*.[18]

The strategies of top management are aimed at the consistent strengthening of the core abilities which set the company apart, and at optimal congruence with the demands of the market/customers. In other words, successful corporate strategies which lead to strategic, that is, not just to short-term, tactical competitive advantages are based on two components: first, on the selection of products or product characteristics

or services which from the point of view of the customer are particularly suitable for setting the company apart; and second, on the knowledge about these characteristics and the targeted support of the company's own specific competences to realise these products or services. Only the combination of both factors ensures success.

At the start of a transformation process, rational arguments and considerations are the main focus. The aim is to define the core elements in need of change, analyse the factors at work, compare developments, and make as objective as possible an assessment. Contents, costs, the length of the change process and the central question of how the changes to be addressed will impact on the relationship with customers are the elements which preoccupy management in this initial phase. At the end of it, the first conclusions are reached regarding the urgency and primary direction of the action.

In the second phase, the factual changes are addressed, expressed in new objectives and often verified and justified with process and product benchmarks. In nearly every instance, the aim is to maintain or regain competitive ability. At the end of this phase, top management justifies the necessity of the changes using the results of the analysis and sets new, quantitative targets. At this time, middle management is actively incorporated into the change process, and is required to act on its own initiative. Identification with the new objectives can only be achieved through comprehensive participation. The preferred means of agreeing new guidelines by consensus is through workshops, in which those involved take on an active role.

Changes Require Full Commitment and Openness

At this point, the third and really critical phase of the whole change process kicks in. The specified objectives can only be achieved if it is possible to secure the full commitment of middle management and a new openness to changes among all those affected. There is no patent formula for the best way of going about things. To put it in abstract and deliberately exaggerated terms, a radical polarisation becomes apparent, which my colleague Jürgen Peddinghaus has graphically and accurately described using the key phrases 'Power of Fire' and 'Power of Water'.

'Power of Fire' can be the method of choice in extreme crises and in turnaround situations – in situations where no time is available for change processes which are prepared for the long term and carefully introduced. If the situation demands urgent action to ensure the survival of the business, as, for example, in the case of Metallgesellschaft (MG) or recently with Holzmann AG, then there is no longer any opportunity to involve management in a planned process of winning people over. To put it bluntly: they have to do what the boss is convinced is right. And anyone who doesn't go along with it should start looking for a new job. Classic turnaround managers obey the clear principle of the rigorously applied Think – Talk – Do approach (see Chapter 4). They have a management style which is characterised by directness, an ability not to be diverted, the exercise of power and short-termism. In certain situations, however, the hard hand of the out-and-out restructurer is the only alternative, as was prescribed for Metallgesellschaft (now MG Technologies) by former Deutsche Bank manager and head of the MG supervisory board Ronaldo Schmitz and Dr Karl Josef (Kajo) Neukirchen following its failed speculation on oil. In such instances, restructuring is simply saving the business from going under. Turnaround generally involves more than this, because it is aimed at the medium and long term.

While all experience suggests that the practice of 'change by shock' has more negative than positive effects when viewed from a medium or long-term perspective, sometimes it is effective as a first phase. The shock only has a short-term impact, and evokes fears and uncertainty; 'rule by fear' only evinces defensive attitudes and moves to bail out. However, having sympathy and a gentle approach over everything similarly gives the wrong signals. In both instances, there is no 'jolt' to shake up the company, and no one is swept along in a move towards new horizons. The key criterion for any attempted change is that it has lasting effect; in other words, one is talking of that lasting change which takes effect beyond the moment of fear. However, restructurers are often unaware that they are on the wrong track if they fail to change their formulae after the initial phase and it is then too late.

By contrast, the 'Power of Water' relies on an open management culture where everyone is fully aware of 'the direction in which the current is heading'. The objective and the direction of the current are not an issue. Extending the metaphor, the water is given time to wash

away the blockages in the flow, instead of blowing them out of the water. Change takes place almost unnoticed, and can only be recognised some time later, perhaps only several years later. Businesses which have become aware at an early stage of the necessity for change and have understood how change is like a steady current have been able to use the 'Power of Water' with great success. 3M, Hewlett Packard, Motorola, Beiersdorf, Henkel or Mannesmann are impressive historical examples. These companies acted early and, using constant change processes, have achieved a position where they avoided experiencing crisis situations, when only radical measures could have guaranteed the continued survival of the company. With the application of the 'Power of Water', a corporate culture is developed and nurtured which can be compared to a regular fitness programme. A corporate culture of this kind allows the performance principle to thrive and nurtures the objective of a carefully balanced stakeholder value, which includes customer value and shareholder value.

With its far-reaching transformation to become a telecommunications group, Mannesmann is (and has been for a long time) an example to show that making radical changes and directing corporate attention to completely new areas of business can be achieved using the 'Power of Water', without the need for breaches and reproaches within the company; that remains true, regardless of the recent upheaval in takeover battles which is without precedent in Germany. Not every transformation process needs to, or will, turn out to be as radical as that at Mannesmann, which led to the spinning-off of the business areas for automotive and plant and machine construction, or (to give a second example) at Preussag, which within a few years has transformed itself from a group operating in coal, iron, steel and raw materials and plant and machine construction into a consumption-linked tourism business of international scale – a process driven by former West-LB CEO Friedel Neuber and Preussag Board Chairman Michael Frenzel.

2.2 People as The Driving Force – Energising Others

Whether it is the hard hand or radical change in sectors and ways of thinking, in every instance successful group restructuring presupposes on

the one hand a high level of technical competence in terms of content, with a deep understanding of markets, trends and the competition, allied with a great deal of internal expertise. On the other hand, it also requires systematic, co-ordinated progress with a solid methodical approach, central programme management and a stringent schedule – three characteristics which Booz Allen Hamilton has also used in its transformation initiative. At the same time, these are three characteristics which place people at their heart, and at all levels.

Transformation is 'a bosses' thing'. The most important success factor for transformation projects is therefore that the leadership role of the board in the change process is clearly determined and visibly communicated to everyone in the company. In practical terms, the management board convenes a steering committee under the chairmanship of a board member. Of course, he or she must have the support of the board chairman. All important decision-makers – which of course include the works councillors (under the German legal provisions for co-determination) – must be involved at an early stage, which means from the very outset that all activities are co-ordinated by a central programme management group. Of course, this management group often also involves external experts in the course of the programme, because with their 'outsider's view' they see many things with a clearer focus, with less prejudice, and on the basis of similar problems encountered in their practical cross-sectoral and cross-company experience. This enables them to bring in industrial, methodical, and above all, objective expertise and necessarily approach the issues with a higher degree of objectivity. Integrity is the indispensable precondition for consultancy; clarity and openness in working with the company and its employees make an essential contribution to success.

A further success factor is a point which has already been briefly mentioned: centrally controlled communication, both internally and externally. I have already stated that change processes generate disquiet and fear, and unfortunately they also heighten receptiveness to the wildest of rumours. As a result, early and open information and a readiness to engage in dialogue at all levels of management are vital contributions to the success of the venture. Taking people within the company seriously means first and foremost informing them, communicating with them, and doing this as intensively as possible. In doing so, consis-

tency in the statements being made is vital. A company can only ever speak with one voice. Anything else, however well meant it might be, is registered negatively as being 'two-faced' by those affected, who have become sensitive to the situation.

Top management must succeed in achieving 'buy-in' by the various levels of management in order to turn them into followers and, ideally, into change agents. In the pursuit of flatter hierarchies and leaner structures, where levels of management are up for review and there are threats to positions which have been laboriously built up, with all the influence and respect attached to them, one may expect the strongest resistance to changes in middle management particularly, unless a culture of transparency where open discussion and latent readiness to change among those in positions of responsibility exists, has already been developed.

Middle Managers Need Satisfying Tasks and Prospects

In my experience as a consultant, and that of my colleagues in many countries around the world, middle management can be recruited for change, despite all the fears and the lack of courage to take decisions, if change can be experienced as an opportunity for success, both personally and as part of a team. Middle managers expect practical, satisfying and lasting tasks which offer them professional opportunities and give them respect, recognition and chances of promotion in the company. They want to see that their effort is recognised, acknowledged and appropriately valued. In other words, top management can only get through the middle level, often referred to as the 'clay layer', successfully if it makes it clear at an early stage whether middle managers individually or as a group have a future in the company, and what that future looks like. Top management should also not shy away from being consistent in letting go anyone who is an opponent of change.

From this finding, an insight can be derived which at first sight may appear to have no regard at all for the people factor, but which in reality has precisely the opposite effect: anyone who has no future in a company must leave that company quickly. The wholly insensitive thing to do is to keep hidden from a manager that he or she has no future in the company. That said, however logical and appropriate their decisions

are, top managers must accept that the termination of a contract should also be experienced and handled as a termination of loyalty to the company. Afterwards, companies no longer have any claim to loyalty on the part of the employee. For modern personnel managers, it goes without saying that the break will be handled with respect for the person involved, and cleanly in terms of its material aspects. Outsourcing and compensation arrangements can only alleviate the situation, not prevent it. The most difficult thing, in personal terms, and the most dangerous aspect for the company, is that where people see no future for themselves, they lapse into a sense of hopelessness. In crisis situations, hopelessness spreads like a plague through economic enterprises. There is no vaccine against it. To extend the metaphor, rapid amputation is the best preventative measure against the danger of infection.

Competent Staff Are at the Heart

Experiences from supporting a large number of businesses through change processes have shown that this process must be generated from above and below at the same time. It cannot be stated often enough that transformation is management's responsibility. Without the full commitment of management, there will be no change. Management must create the preconditions, it must want to make the change apparent for everyone across the whole process chain, it must defend that change and live it for itself. In the change process, above all, top management can build on the layer of employees who are competence carriers, on the readiness to change of those people who are the real 'adders of value' in the value-added chain in development, manufacturing, procurement, marketing and customer services. Experienced practitioners are aware that these employees know the necessary parameters to be able to work efficiently, productively, creatively, meaningfully. And in most instances they know very clearly what and who is obstructing them in this. The 'competent staff', as they have been termed by Jürgen Peddinghaus, Chairman of the Senior Advisory Board of Booz Allen Hamilton Germany, form the heart of corporate knowledge and corporate abilities. Their competence, which admittedly needs to be subject to constant development if it is not to fossilise, is what makes the future.

It is absolutely vital that management levels are won over for the change. But that alone is not enough. The change process must encompass the whole staff. As already suggested, this is mainly a question of communication. Print media such as the company magazine, and even internal company television (where available) are only suitable for this purpose to a limited extent, because the opportunity to convince people lies in person-to-person dialogue. Even in instances where a large number of employees are involved, this must not be an obstacle to pursuing the laborious and time-consuming route of personal, one-to-one and group communications. To do this requires a comprehensive communications concept, using the cascade principle to reach all employees. This communication process has three clearly defined goals. When it is completed, employees should:

■ Be convinced of the need for change

■ Accept the change

■ Actively drive forward the change process.

Among the essential preconditions for acceptance of values-oriented management in the change process – a point which I cannot emphasise enough – is precisely planned, intensive, open communication delivered in a personal dialogue, which simultaneously increases the credibility of and confidence in management. It encompasses contents, costs, quality and times as well as successes by way of improvement, but similarly it covers deficiencies or reversals. Commitment from the competent staff, particularly at the ground level, can only be achieved with such genuinely open and personally conducted communication. This also means that communication intended to reach the ground level must be carried out in their language, in the language of the target group. The language, the figures of speech, the arguments and conclusions must be understood. The language sometimes derisively termed 'management-speak' is as out of place in this context as complexly generated ratios and unintelligible graphics.

Dialogue with the second and the third tier of management is important. Programmes must be prepared which do not avoid addressing the more problematic questions for these managers. In doing so, the

programme should not only address the questions about what those being managed expect of management or how management is fulfilling expectations, but, for example, it should also address how the manager sees himself and how those whom he manages view him. What must be discovered is how internal and external customers and partners of the company view the management at these levels and the services which they provide. Finally, the question also needs to be asked about how the conduct of the leaders in the team is judged by the team members, and what consequences arise from that.

Clear Answers to Problematic Questions

The prospects for success of this communication process are greater the more the system of values is identifiable and comprehensible for employees – that canon of values on which the thinking, decision-making and actions of top management are based. A sober and inviolable store of values which survives as a fixed link through all phases of change renders the actions of management predictable for employees. Admittedly, that store of values only becomes credible when the actions of top managers are demonstrably in accord with it. So-called 'quick fixes' are a good way to achieve this – so long as things progress beyond this. In workshops with a healthy mix of 'hierarchs' and 'competents', issues which are susceptible to a quick fix delivering short-term solutions and results can be discussed. The teams communicate their solutions to management, justify them and expect rapid decisions as proof of the willingness of management to change. In pursuing this approach, it is not recommended to start with too many or too complicated issues simulta-neously, since then the danger of not achieving anything is too great. If senior management wants to turn those who 'wait-and-see' into followers, fears into self-confidence, risk-aversity into a readiness to accept responsibility, and a 'safety-first' philosophy into a readiness to take risks, then it must define and secure binding agreement on values and consistently respect those values, while also consistently demanding similar respect for them from all levels of management.

Values-based management is an issue of huge importance for the change process, because it is critical to success. At the same time, it

goes far beyond the special problems relating to the change process as discussed here; it encompasses all areas of company management. For that reason, values-based management is of key importance for the CEO agenda – not least in the face of the social context facing businesses at the start of the third millennium. This aspect has already been addressed in section 1.6. In section 3.4 the complex relationships between the system of values, corporate culture and corporate success are discussed.

Energising/Increasing Human Potential

The objective of transformation is, in general terms, the energising of the whole company with the overarching objective of motivating and activating human potential. Of course, ultimately it is about an improvement in the hard factors. In the final phase of the process, the change in performance which is achieved must be measured, analysed and developed further. Contents, costs, quality and times must be clearly measurable. For this, a system of performance measurement must be put in place which is designed to be specific to the company, for example a balanced scorecard system. Systematic rigour is also required in the financial and personal recognition of services, to do justice to the fundamental values of fairness, acceptance, proper conduct, dignity and trust, which are always the bottom line when dealing with people. Courage must be rewarded – this is an important rule in the change process – to encourage the 'wait-and-sees' and develop them into followers. The old truism similarly holds good here: nothing succeeds like success. Measurable successes attract further successes in their wake, success breeds success. Followers develop into change champions, and the process gains its own dynamism. The hard factors themselves then automatically change with increasing speed in a positive direction.

On the one hand, the change process is directed at achieving the necessary flexibility to survive in the face of the competition, but it is simultaneously aimed at the maintenance and optimal use of synergies. To that end, Booz Allen Hamilton has developed the model of the centreless corporation. Under that concept, the traditional group headquarters is slimmed down to a lean global core and strategic manage-

ment of the business units. This new group head office retains only a few central core tasks. The organisation and the method of working are redefined as part of this change.

Corporate activity in the market is managed by the customer-oriented business units (see section 2.4). The shared services support the market-focused units with services which they perform for all the business units together, cost-effectively and to a high quality standard. The following sections are devoted to these core elements of the flexible company and its organisational arrangement.

2.3   Refashioning The Centre – The Centreless Corporation

Given the key challenges of globalisation and the increasing complexity of I-World, company managements see themselves exposed to further increasing competitive pressure. To withstand this competitive pressure, consistent orientation on the customer's needs and an energetic ability to innovate are the most likely strategies to achieve success. The dominant internal and external influencing factors lead, of necessity, to changed emphases for tasks. Traditional organisational structures no longer appear suitable for solving pressing problems. This always affects the individual particularly.

A refashioning of the group headquarters, reducing it to its core functions, is on the one hand the logical response to the radically altered profile of requirements. On the other hand, this refashioning is a logical consequence of the possibilities afforded by modern information and communications technologies, which have probably for the first time ever made management of flexible, decentralised company structures in a global federation a possibility. At the same time, these technologies are one of the preconditions (even if by no means the only precondition) for goal-oriented use of the knowledge existing within the company; and today, more clearly than ever before, it is acknowledged how important this is for the survival and success of the company. Only the learning organisation is suited to activating this knowledge, to generating new knowledge and converting this into as steady as possible a flow of innovations. Section 3.7 is devoted to the issues of knowledge management and competence domains.

For a knowledge-based, learning company with flat hierarchies which makes consistent use of the constant advances in information and communications technologies, the transition from a traditional, old-style centralised organisation with hierarchical features to the new corporate shape of the extended enterprise is a logical move. Under this arrangement, a networked horizontal organisation links suppliers, partners, customers, universities, institutes, and service providers of all kinds closely with one another. Geographical distances become almost meaningless, since with information transfer via the Internet or internal company Intranets, not only does the importance of distance diminish, but so does the amount spent on communication costs. It is apparent to anyone that a structure as complex and complicated as the extended enterprise demands a specific management and organisational structure with a high degree of delegated responsibility. At the same time, it means that interesting jobs are formed right across the widely branching organisation, where employees are able to use their abilities and develop their talents.

Adding Value is the Prime Task of the Global Core

'A core, not a centre' is one of the key statements which Bruce A. Pasternack[19] uses in describing the departure from the traditional, 'all-knowing' and all-controlling company headquarters:

> The true test for the role of the global core is that it is the heart and the corner-stone of the company, making it more valuable than the sum of its parts. The matter is simple and straightforward: its role is to add value ... Any other role negates value.

The management of the global core concentrates on corporate strategy, on the one central task of achieving added value beyond the level of that which the business units achieve or are capable of realising:

> The strategy should be based on the strategic question of why the different parts of the organisation should come together to collectively assume a leading position in the first place. It is a very dynamic and positive role –

one which, if approached correctly, should be recognised as positive for the whole company.

Of course, this approach also combines with the question as to which parts of the company are no longer to be counted as belonging to the strategic core areas and should possibly be spun off from the company. The global core must create its value in a networked world. Pasternack explains with emphasis:

> It goes without saying that the role of the global core is important. It is the corner-stone of the Centreless Corporation. If it is not successful, the essential purpose of the Centreless Corporation cannot be achieved.[19]

Consistent with the concept of the extended enterprise, the global core produces added value where the business units cannot, for example by arranging the business portfolio, through strategic support for individual businesses, by intensifying the knowledge transfer between company units and realising unexploited synergy potentials across several business areas. The rules are strict. Under this arrangement the burden of proof for this additional added value lies clearly with the group management.

The fact that adding value is the primary task of the global core should already be sufficiently apparent. Beyond that, delegation and decentralisation of tasks and responsibilities are the strategic tasks for the group management. Its objective must be:

- To develop customer orientation into a lived culture across the whole company;

- To generate cost-awareness at all levels – beginning with the global core itself;

- To attune the company to speed in all its processes and to rapid implementation;

- To give employees more independence, to empower them to act independently, to motivate them;

- To seek to provide better quality of life for the individual within the company.

It is the Duty of the Top Manager to Develop Human Potential

Caring about the people in the company, in the sense of providing help in the development of the potential of the individual, is an important element in the list of duties of the top manager.

The group management itself is responsible for ensuring that it defines its global and cross-disciplinary tasks and credibly presents itself as indispensable to the parts of the company.

The strategic core tasks of the global core can be described using five concepts:

- Strategic management

- Identity

- Strategic control

- Capital

- Competence.

Strategic management is concentrated on defining values which are valid and binding across the group, and on identifying growth potential outside the day-to-day business and across the business areas. This also includes support and co-ordination of major change processes.

Identity describes in summary form the development of the corporate identity and its communication to staff and the public, also taking into account local/cultural conditions. This strategic area of work also includes representing the company to shareholders, the authorities and employees.

Strategic control serves to aid representation of the interests of share-holders and stakeholders overall, provides the supervisory board with the necessary data to exercise its governance function arising from the constant monitoring of strategic and financial risks. Strategic control-ling comprises the definition, prescription and monitoring of consistent key performance figures across all business units, the analysis and assessment of business results, and the avoidance of harmful effects from internal competition between individual businesses. This service helps with conflict resolution.

Capital is the keyword for the tasks of the global core in the area of finance. Of these, the most important is the task of minimising capital costs. Other tasks include securing loan capital and equity capital, together with effective risk management, treasury management and liquidity management.

Competence reflects the oft mentioned, steadily increasing importance of knowledge for the success of the company. In practical terms, this involves the – pooled – gathering and dissemination of best practice skills, central innovation management (insofar as this is sensible and not more effectively located within the business areas), and knowledge management, including co-ordination of the competence domains, whose function is explained in section 3.7. This category also includes central legal and IT functions.

The chairman of the board for the centreless corporation is confronted with a series of challenges and problems in his global core function, the most important of which I consider to be the definition and determining of the agenda, here taken as meaning the programme, the list of issues and tasks. This is the point at which the direction is determined and all the activities which follow are co-ordinated. Immediately below this on the scale of priorities comes the building up and the development of the management team. Having an operational grip on the company, really taking hold of the business, and building up relationships with the most important partners, customers and suppliers, the shareholders and the trades unions deserve equal weighting on this list, to my mind. In this way, the group can extract optimal benefit from the skills developed in the business units close to the market.

In the traditional business model with a strong headquarters, the group management was allocated numerous staff functions, including purchasing and researching information systems, human resources, governance, the legal, tax and finance departments and press and publicity work. In the new model of the lean, flexible business with a global core, large parts of these staff functions are located in the business units, or they are positioned as company-wide services – the so-called shared services.

Philips Electronics is an interesting example of the logical development of global core thinking. The company has – courageously – freed its former group headquarters from the immediate surroundings of the

corporate areas, laboratories and factories in its traditional location in Eindhoven, and located its new, lean management unit in Amsterdam.

Targeted Bundling of Usefully Shared Elements

Despite all the evident advisability of displacing functions from the old-style headquarters to the business units, there are nevertheless a number of common services, the so-called shared services, which should be located neither in the head office nor in the business units, but which instead form a separate category outside the global core. A simple decision tree with seven sequential key points enables these necessary company-wide services to be defined with ease:

1. To define the boundaries of the global core, it should be asked whether the activity under discussion falls under one of the five strategic core tasks of the global core.

2. If this is not the case, the next question is: do the business units need this service as internal customers?

3. If the answer is no, then it is reasonable to disband the relevant service.

4. If the answer is yes, then the next question is whether this service delivers a competitive advantage.

5. If the answer is yes, the decision remains open as to whether this service can be better provided through incorporation into the business units or by being allocated to the common services.

6. If there is no clearly identifiable competitive advantage, management must ask itself whether third parties external to the company could provide this service more cost-effectively and/or better. In deciding this, 'better' must also mean that safety, confidentiality, reliability, and identification with the business is guaranteed at least as clearly as if the service remains within the business.

7. However, if outsourcing does not bring any advantages, then the final question relates to the economies of scale if the function is allocated

to the shared services. If there are no such economies of scale, then it seems reasonable to assume that incorporation into the business units is more advantageous.

At the end of this series of decisions, it is also apparent that shared services are only entitled to exist if they support the global core and the business units with services which are appropriate for the market. To that end, company-wide services must work in accordance with five core principles:

- Shared services demand price transparency. Every service has its price. The business units decide which services they will buy in at this price.

- Management runs the services as a genuine 'business' with responsibility for results, and not as a cost centre.

- For shared services, market orientation means attending to the wishes of its internal customers. It is not a question of what shared services departments consider to be correct, but of what the customers want.

- The services are subject to the principle of best practice, which means that they must allow themselves to be measured against the market, both internally and externally.

- The process of providing services must be flexible, and capable of rapid implementation.

The daily experience of business life shows that the high demands made of common, company-wide services only find acceptance in the long term in those areas where there is recognisably the same desire for a particular service within the various business units. Very careful attention should be paid to ensuring that measurements of performance are not made using two different yardsticks. Otherwise excessive pressure on the 'supplier' of the service results in demotivation similar to the 'Lopez effect' which the Spanish manager caused among a considerable number of VW suppliers during his time as head of purchasing.

In connection with the subject of this book, one aspect of the development outlined here seems particularly important: with the centreless corporation, and with careful management of the essential factors by the global core, major opportunities open up for people within the company for independent thinking and action under the individual's own responsibility. Or, to formulate this more precisely: unless there is a deep trust in this independence, in this readiness to accept responsibility and risk on the part of employees in the extended enterprise, the new business model can neither be imagined nor realised.

The number of managers operating on an international basis, in particular, has increased markedly in the course of globalisation and with the development of decentralised structures. At the same time as responsibility is moving away from the old-style company headquarters and into the operating units, the influence of these managers has become significantly larger and, consequently, they have more responsibility. Josep Franch and Kamran Kashani, Professors of Marketing in Barcelona and Lausanne respectively, have described the principal spectrum of tasks being taken on by these types of international manager.[20] These managers are responsible in the relevant company areas/business areas for formulating regional or global strategies for a business or a function. They are also responsible for aligning local activities with the regional or the global strategies (the latter being the responsibility of the global core). With regard to the individual business area, their tasks include the integration and co-ordination of initiatives in different national organisations for a common objective. Franch and Kashani see a further task as effecting a reduction in those activities which are replicated in several local organisations (and which can possibly be performed better and more cost-effectively by shared services). Furthermore – and by no means the least of their tasks – they should identify best practice and transfer these to other countries. In other words: beneath the global core management, they are responsible for very similar tasks to those of top management.

Just as for the international managers at business unit level, as described above, the complexity of the tasks in the global core demands a selective procedure pursuing clear and above all strategic priorities, which still leave sufficient room for manoeuvre for the respective local management. At the same time, it is important that no new moves to

bureaucratise the system develop alongside the new decentralised and flexible structures. Jack Welch, the successful former CEO of GE, sees the danger of bureaucratic fossilisation as one of the core problems of modern organisations. In his own emphatic style of expression, he observes: 'Fight bureaucracy in the company! Hate it! Kick it up the ass! Break it!'[21] You cannot put it more clearly than that. And doing away with bureaucracy is a natural human inclination.

2.4 Operating in Manageable Units: Decentralisation and Destructuring

Business structures are not made 'for all eternity'. They are constantly changing. Major companies, as can be seen from numerous examples worldwide, develop their organisational structures in waves which ebb and flow between the two poles of centralisation and decentralisation. It may very well be the case that this change at least keeps the businesses and the people working within them alert and guards against fossilisation, and that the fact of the movement itself is more important than the direction in which it takes the company.

Lovers of plays on words could easily link destructuring to the question as to whether this is actually a destructive process. Destructuring, however, primarily means breaking up, thinning out and trimming existing structures, while at the same time strengthening autonomy. I would only wish to term destructuring as destructive in those instances where either the existing structures are viewed solely and uncritically as positive, or where structures are to be completely eliminated. If existing structures are felt to be limiting for the development of the company, then destructuring is a positive process. Nevertheless, the term remains open to misinterpretation. Debureaucratisation is probably the more unambiguous concept, less open to misinterpretation, and one which better matches the actual objective, at least in Germany. At any rate, today in most companies there are still far too many bureaucratic processes, determined by structures and hierarchies, which hinder the success of the company because they allow too little space in which independent thinking by employees can flourish. It starts from the failure to include people in the information flow. Only informed employees can make correct decisions.

Values such as tolerance and the ability to communicate a sense of self-worth are among the essential qualities for achieving this management task.

Incidentally, another element which also forms a part of lean structures was described pithily and tellingly in August 1999 in the joking remark made by Axel Pfeil, the Head of Management Holdings at Deutsche Bank for its non-banking investments and a supervisor to, by then, 21 employees: 'No drivers, no tea-boys, no doormen, no bodyguards.'

Working in Manageable Structures

Daniel Goeudevert, an always challenging ex-board member at Renault, Ford and latterly with VW, explains quite explicitly, on the grounds of his own experience, where he sees the weaknesses of the traditional structures in major companies: major structures are not able to survive unless they are sub-divided internally. The successful mega-groups of the future will be managed like small family businesses: 'Working people want an overview, orientation and leadership in a clear structure ... Even major company groups should again give a human face to management.'[22] That sounds like a romantic throwback to a past world, but it contains elements which can be transferred to the present day. In this context, giving a human face to management can only mean that management figures live out the values, thereby acquiring an authority which is not dependent on the power inherent in holding a position within a hierarchy. The idea of elected leaders, which today seems to smack of Utopia, – in the sense that they have been accepted by employees – is given very real substance in the light of these reflections.

Decentralisation is aimed primarily at forming smaller, manageable units, which can in fact be managed like family businesses – that is, with a very flat hierarchy – and can therefore work as market engines in an aggressive and wholly customer-centric manner. As has already been demonstrated, these units require a high level of autonomy and independence in order to satisfy local circumstances and specificities. The market engines are the indispensable complementary element to the global core. They can only operate at full speed with the optimal

level of efficiency if the company's top management in the global core respects their independence, instead of attempting to tell them how to run their day-to-day business.

Conversely, the business areas and their managements must also redefine their role, to go beyond traditional group egotisms and empire-building tendencies. They must have flexible access, across organisational boundaries, to knowledge and skills in the whole company group, and not be sucked into a 'not invented here' mentality. And in return they must unreservedly make available their own skills, their knowledge of markets and customers. It is part of the role of the global core to initiate, instil and promote this new, open behaviour. To put it another way, the managements of business units and business fields are themselves responsible for looking over the parapet. Extended responsibilities for the business units also impact – very clearly so – on responsibility towards the business as a whole. The task is as follows: business units must make a contribution to adding value across the whole system, independently of one another and going beyond their respective individual performance capability. By exchanges and networking, they must offer mutual support in producing their added value, thereby overcoming the danger of defensive empire-building.

In other words: to open up or exploit new opportunities for growth effectively, there is a need for group-wide, flexible, horizontal co-operation between the individual business units, that is, the people working in them, without the need for installing new matrix structures with all their familiar problems, created above all by internal friction. The decisive factor is that the core abilities identified group-wide are transferred between the business units without any negative impact from a 'unit mentality', and that internal benchmarking facilitates the identification and cross-unit implementation of best practice. Organisations whose units learn from one another and continually raise the internal standards by which they measure themselves will quickly overhaul the competition, and can achieve leading positions in the market. At the same time, a 'knowledge competition' is generated within the business which can liberate new forces.

In this model of the autonomously operating manageable unit, working in harmony with the wider whole, *informed employees become part of the shared vision*. The successful decentralised businesses of the

future, which are already being realised today in a number of instances, will nurture a culture of shared knowledge and will be prepared to disseminate this knowledge to all those who need it. This will happen, as has already been mentioned, irrespective of functional and/or regional boundaries. This new attitude of openness and readiness to co-operate is also necessary, in my opinion, for successful knowledge management. To be able to take good decisions quickly and develop innovative solutions, employees in their new autonomous environment in the centreless corporation need more information, less supervision, and a deeper shared sense of the corporate mission. Nearly two-thirds of first-level management who took part in a study of the effects of the Internet on business are aware of the need to empower their better-informed employees to exercise greater freedom to take decisions. In return, they expect a positive change in their organisations which will lead to competitive advantages. This will make the paradigm shift from the skilled individual entrepreneur of the past to the compatible network of interdisciplinary individual functions a reality.

It is certainly true that traditional business structures were always able to give the individual a certain measure of security. For many reasons, this security has become precarious and at the same time a key issue. If security is largely lost, then only better education and training can provide individuals with a degree of counterbalance. Only in this way can individuals recognise the dangers at an early stage and react to them appropriately. Better training is therefore an essential condition for a successful process of destructuring. The new corporate reality being brought about by targeted destructuring, and the new and higher demands which this brings for employees required to participate in the thinking process, represent an immense challenge for every business, for every top management and for our education system as a whole.

2.5 The Benefits of Networks – Scalable Size

The success of economic activity will increasingly depend on whether companies succeed in using network structures and developing into global networks. In the extended enterprise of the 21st century, it is more important to be optimally networked than to cement membership

of a corporate group through capital links which one may possibly have to break apart again tomorrow if new opportunities and projects demand new forms of arrangement. Network-like links are less ponderous than command pyramids, as the American sociologist Walter Powell recognised at an early stage; flexible institutions can be reorganised or even, if necessary, dissolved more easily than rigid hierarchies. In section 1.2 the role played by the Internet and the World Wide Web in the development of networks as catalysts and accelerators has already been outlined. However, it is ultimately the ability to manage networks which determines the economic success of these networks, together with the ability of the company to innovate. In this regard, the reader is also referred to section 2.6. The rapid increase in networking within and between businesses opens up a broad field of applications for network-based multimedia solutions.

Also Applicable to Institutional Areas – e-Government Initiatives are Clear Evidence

Applications range from video-conferencing through teleworking and telelearning to multimedia kiosk systems. Former Intel CEO Andy Grove has declared:

> The Internet takes the information exchange between the parts of a company and its partners to a higher level, because it connects networks which up until that point had been operating independently. It is a kind of *lingua franca* for global communication.[23]

The Internet does indeed usher in a new global marketplace. Customers around the world are becoming increasingly demanding. At all times, day or night, they want products and services which are precisely tailored to their requirements, they expect to get this service at a good price and they are only too aware that the next competitor is waiting for them only a mouse-click away. Some 84 per cent of businesses, a clear majority of those interviewed about the issue of the importance of the Internet, believe that the Internet is accelerating the trend towards globalisation of their companies. The Internet is chal-

lenging them to transform their strategies, their organisation and their processes and, beyond that, in many instances to renew their whole approach to business. The possibility of increasing revenues through direct contact with the customer is at first sight the foremost application, within a very much larger phenomenon. Such initiatives help businesses to increase their market share and improve results, but along with this they can also achieve massive cost savings in reducing their inventories and logistics costs by rethinking their processes and their relationships; but above all, however, the benefits lie in getting to know their customers better. This ability to network efficiently with everyone – customers, suppliers, service providers, employees and partners – changes the entire basis of the competition. For CEOs, this results in the need to develop new and more radical business models to enable their companies to compete effectively in the I-World. They must respond to the changed situation with new strategies, using Internet strategies as a lever and preparing their businesses for e-Business and new forms of organisation.

Managing External Relationships

For the dominating role of networks in future, SAP CEO Hasso Plattner offers a very simple justification, which coincides precisely with the statements taken from the CEO survey and quoted above: 'It is no longer only internal organisation which determines one's success in the market, but above all the efficient management of external relationships with suppliers, co-operation partners and customers.'[24] In other words, the decisive factors are the management and co-ordination of the extended enterprise – driven forward to manage cross-company business processes, including through the use of new software technologies, with those processes in turn providing the new profile of requirements for these complex software developments, in an interdependent and repeating process. Businesses must reinvent themselves. Good examples of consistent use of the Internet can be found in Germany today. BMW, for example, is one of the earliest and most progressive users of the Internet as a marketing tool in the end-customer area. It is estimated that 70–80 per cent of buyers who order a BMW 7 series vehicle have

previously obtained information via the Internet. In the business-to-business area, the ball-bearing manufacturer FAG Kugelfischer used Internet technologies to integrate the company into the supplier systems of its customers – particularly in the automotive and aviation industry – in such a manner that it became a partner, and one who is present every step of the way, so to speak.

At the same time, internal organisational networking remains a vital precondition for corporate success. It is self-evident that a learning organisation, equipped with experience of knowledge management, can perform this task far better than an organisation operating along traditional lines. Optimised organisational networking includes a multiplicity of internal relationships, such as the following:

- Between strategic guidelines and daily management decisions or measures;

- Between the defined full performance potential of the business on the one hand and the negotiated/agreed goals of managers as the result of the planning and budgeting process on the other;

- Between financial results and operational obligations on the one hand and more far-reaching management decisions on the other;

- Between business managements and other management levels;

- Between horizontal, functional and operational units;

- Between line management and finance and control departments;

- Between management decisions (as cause) and financial results (as consequence);

- Between the point in time when new insights about the future (for example as the result of intensive knowledge management) are acquired, and the point in time when the operational management decisions are adapted to take account of these insights;

- Between the areas under a person's authority and incentive systems for managers on the one hand, and the decisions for which they are responsible on the other.

If organisational networking is established to correspond to this profile of requirements, then it makes it possible for the entire management to pursue common objectives across all functions and operating units as a result of the new transparency which is achieved. Management can concentrate on the really important decisions which lead to a change in operational parameters, that is, of major and decisive importance in terms of the ability to compete. Only a logical cycle encompassing relevant findings, measures leading to particular objectives, accurate performance measurement and motivating reward structures can energise the business flow and help the company to achieve that flexibility and speed of reaction which secures its survival in the global competition of the knowledge society.

Challenging Positions – New Opportunities in Networks

Management and employees find numerous challenging and multifaceted, and therefore satisfying, positions in such networks, offering them the chance to further develop their skills and personal expertise. In the long term, this new definition of the relationship between the employee and the company offers more security for the future than the deceptive 'job security' in old, rigid hierarchies. Admittedly, networks only fulfil their function if and when they connect people in the company and in the extended enterprise, and not only in the technical sense. The aim is to have a lively exchange of information whose horizontal and vertical flows run 'top down' and 'bottom up'. Human networks neither come into existence 'on command', nor grow very fast. Building them up can, however, be activated, accelerated and invigorated by group-wide exchange programmes for competence carriers. ABB has had good experiences from its efforts in this regard, for example. The intellectual base of the organisation became significantly wider as a result of the exchange of knowledge and experiences between people from parts of the company all over the world. The communications processes are being simplified and accelerated, and decision-making paths are becoming shorter.

In the past decade, the concentration on core businesses and core competences has been the most important driver behind company consolidations, takeovers and mergers. By contrast, in the 1980s, inte-

gration along the value-added chain was the most important impulse behind the wave of consolidations. In the 1970s, a completely different paradigm dictated the takeover strategies of company groups, namely the notion of distributing risk by forming conglomerates. The old ITT under Harold Geneen was the classic example of this.

With the development of competence networks, companies are now realising a new dimension in knowledge management. So-called competence domains constitute the intellectual interfaces of such networks, as virtual teams in which competence carriers/knowledge workers collaborate on an interdisciplinary basis, without the barriers of hierarchy, across areas and across company boundaries. The way in which these competence domains work, collaborate and are organised is explained in section 3.7.

Companies aspire to greater size – and often for good reason – and for the size which is measured by the global market. On the other hand, however, they need to remain close to their customers to ensure their further growth. Clearly these equally important business objectives do not go hand in hand. On the contrary, resolving the contradiction between size and closeness to customers remains a challenge for top management, the solution to which goes deep into the structure of the company. Here we are talking about achieving size through the networking of manageable units, within which that sense of 'us' can develop, as Goeudevert also argues. Ultimately, it is people who are the nodes of these networks. They can only operate if they possess social competence – that ability without which the manager of today and tomorrow is inconceivable.

The objective is the friction-free interplay of the market-facing units, that is, the units on the ground (whether they are organised in a region, a country or market segment), which work as market engines with high levels of dynamism directly with customers, and the global core or corporate core, that is, the company headquarters, which is still an indispensable element, even if it is much smaller, leaner and reduced to its core functions when compared with the organisational forms of the past. Tasks and processes relating to the customer-oriented units and to the new, slimmed-down headquarters, together with the interfaces between the units, must be defined with great precision, if they are not to become the source of permanent frictions which drain energies and are a drag on efficiency.

Managers are Creating New Dimensions

In global terms, company consolidations and takeovers amounted to a value of €2800 billion in 1999. Of this, €1200 billion or almost 43 per cent took place in Europe.

In the variety of (published) reasons and impulses behind mergers and takeovers, the list of strategic goals being pursued is relatively similar throughout:

- Generating shareholder value;

- Realising the benefits of size (economies of scale);

- Creating synergies;

- Concentration on core businesses (also making use of outsourcing and disinvestment).

Despite the immense wave of mergers and takeovers, large sections of top management view this trend soberly – sometimes with a reticence that borders on scepticism. The high failure rate proves them right in many respects. The number of failed mergers is growing; the list of takeover and merger talks which have been broken off is too long to recount. Thus it is no accident that many business leaders prefer the alternative of organic growth under one's own efforts, and are energetically driving forward this form of expansion with ambitious targets. In the desire for size, these managers argue, it is easily overlooked that size is not the same thing as strength, in the sense of the power to innovate, the ability to market products, and profitability.

However, some managers do not set much store by the popularly contrasted pairings of 'small and fast' versus 'big and slow':

> The right combination is big and fast. If companies are fast, then size is an enormous advantage, making them practically unbeatable.[23]

In a corporate culture where performance capability and readiness to perform enjoy a high priority within the canon of values, ambitious goals are a matter of course. One of the most certain routes to above-

average growth is to drive forward the development of performance capability for the core business consistently and constantly – it is more successful than a hastily contrived diversification into business areas for which the company lacks the relevant core competences.

To implement a growth strategy, determination is required – irrespective of whether this is for internal growth or expansion through acquisitions or mergers. Company boards which fail to show such determination, fail to set themselves and their employees ambitious targets or do not know how to implement such targets in an energetic manner, should not be surprised to experience stagnation or only modest growth.

It Comes Down to the Increase in Value

It goes without saying that growth must go hand in hand with positive contributions to value. Growth without achievable profitability in the medium term leads very quickly to a lasting weakening of the whole company. Today's institutional investors react vigorously to that. Businesses must optimise their specific size to fit the scale of the relevant sector. Energy suppliers, for example, operate in a saturated market with minimal growth of 1.0–1.5 per cent annually. This market has been transformed into a competitive market in a remarkably short period of time, and one which is particularly under pressure from cost-conscious commercial users. If a company wants to grow in a market like this, it is only possible through targeted competition to win market share from the competition, which in the first instance is done on price (and naturally has an impact on the balance sheets). The necessary measures cannot be implemented blindly from a central headquarters, but can only be brought in with careful adjustment to suit the given local/regional markets.

The competition – if it is aiming to drive a company out of the market – can be fought off all the more successfully the bigger the power of the company in the market, and the greater its powers of procurement. These two interdependent factors are largely determined by size. The mergers of VEBA and VIAG, and RWE and VEW show where such considerations lead.

Conglomerates will have to find the scale of the optimal size for each of their specific units. Growth must not be allowed to become a false god! Managers will have to keep in mind that their responsibility increases with every move towards new orders of magnitude. Growth in manageable stages (where one has an eye to what is involved, so to speak) is generally not possible in the context of major mergers, or in genuine or supposed mergers of equals. Every merger means an impetus for growth (and when in doubt, of non-organic growth) and an abrupt rise into new orders of magnitude.

Pitfalls for Mergers

If the people factor truly ranks among the long-term important success factors, then it follows that ultimately only those mergers can be completed successfully which accord appropriate weighting to the aspects which affect individual people. It is no accident that a large number of the mergers of the past years have resulted in greater or lesser degrees of failure. This frequently comes about because there is a gross underestimation of the frictions which arise when two corporate cultures collide. It starts with the managers at the topmost level, and then continues throughout the whole organisation. There are plenty of negative examples of this kind. Moreover, the economic success of many merged companies could be greater and much larger synergy effects could be achieved if, in the process, the prevailing cultures were not destroyed and the human values were not neglected. This is where traditional leadership qualities such as character, tolerance, vision and sensitivity are required.

During the transition from a monopoly to a competitive market, and often later in the consolidation phase, in other words when changes occur which initiate waves of new company formations and mergers in all the sectors affected, one of the primary tasks of management is to create a climate for a competitively oriented corporate culture which is tolerant enough to be able to assimilate and integrate other corporate cultures. Open discussion meetings where the board answers the employees' questions are a proven method of doing this. The new requirements resulting from new functions must be clearly presented to

employees. The employees must understand that they can best secure their professional future in the company by satisfying these requirements proactively. If that is the case, then right from the start they are valuable to the company; accordingly, they are not threatened with redundancy. If employees are carefully taken along on the journey to a new world, then they can also be brought safely through dramatic change processes.

2.6 Winning the Future: Innovations and Creativity

'Research is converting money into knowledge, innovation is converting knowledge into money' is an often-quoted phrase. Schott Research Director Udo Ungeheuer has appropriately added: 'But innovations cannot be prescribed, they must grow and develop.'[25] It is one of the key findings of a Booz Allen Hamilton study on the ability to innovate, conducted in a number of countries, that in addition to sector-specific framework conditions, it is particularly the way in which the company handles the issue of innovation which is definitive in determining the quality and intensity of the power to innovate.

Companies need a climate of openness and liberalness in which their wealth of ideas and creativity can develop. This climate can only be created top down – from the visible commitment, the will and the model set by the company management. Creating this climate is, however, easier said than done. And it presumes that there is a progressively organised innovation management process, which will be addressed here in detail.

To reiterate the point: it is the power to innovate which to a large extent determines corporate success in the currently developing global networks. 'The only thing which counts is the ability of the company to move forward into the future', is how Dr Wendelin Wiedeking, Chairman of the Board at Porsche AG, formulated this same corporate insight at the company's AGM in January 1999.[26] Growth under one's own efforts means above all growth derived from one's own power to innovate. The turnaround at Porsche shows that very impressively. Innovations serve as a critical success factor in competition-rich markets. In such circumstances, margins very quickly come under pres-

sure in the face of ever-shortening product life-cycles, if competitors bring new products onto the market and cause one's own product to appear 'old' long before the originally planned life-cycle ends. In many sectors, a product life-cycle comes to an end after only 18 months, and in the information and communications sector after 12 months at the latest. Only a steady flow of new, innovative products secures sufficiently high profits.

No other sector demonstrates the importance of the power to innovate for the future of the company and its influence on the valuation of the company as directly as the pharmaceuticals industry. The correlation between the research and product pipeline on the one hand and the value of the company/share price on the other could not be closer. Although not so directly apparent, the power to innovate is similarly important in all other competition-rich sectors of industry. And is there any sector which is not competition-rich under globalisation? The product offensives by DaimlerChrysler and the VW Group are only two from numerous recent examples of the strategy of securing the ability to compete through innovations.

With the larger markets for the selling of products which are appearing in the course of globalisation, and not least via the Internet, the readiness of companies to provide research and development with larger budgets grows with increasing economies of scale, thus creating important conditions for innovation. Naturally, investments in research and development are particularly risky. The outcome of research projects is always uncertain, and that uncertainty persists over long time-frames. The work currently being undertaken on fuel cells for the vehicle engine of the future by the Canadian company Ballard Power is a good example of this.

Similarly, there are considerable risks in the development of new kinds of product, in particular where proven approaches are disregarded. The DaimlerChrysler A-Class and the Smart city car show that even highly experienced businesses are not free of such risks. However, rigorously attempting to minimise such risks means possibly missing out on opportunities for innovation. No company can afford to do that, and thus targeted risk management is indispensable, beginning with a precise analysis of the target market. For example, the American pharmaceuticals company Pfizer (known for its Viagra product) attrib-

utes its successes to a considerable extent to very precise definition of the relevant market segment. The company consistently refuses to pursue pharmaceutical developments which do not promise optimal market success – even if this means that it is perhaps not possible to help groups of sufferers which are 'too small' in number.

'A high degree of risk always attaches to innovation processes, which are tough and drawn out – and with every step the stakes get higher', confirms Professor Hans-Jürgen Warnecke, President of the Fraunhofer Gesellschaft.

> That is why aspects like process safety and cost minimisation come to the forefront in the later phases of innovations. Innovation is not a simple linear progression from the invention to the finished product, but a complex inter-play between scientific, technical, economic and social forces.[11]

Innovation is not only a technical process, but also a social and inter-active process.

The market is determined by the desires and values of society. For that reason, the comment which can repeatedly be heard about 'the market not yet being ready for it' is wholly justified in many instances. However, this fact should not be used as a justification for postponing decisions which urgently need to be taken. Aversion to risk is just as dangerous as a lack of willingness to take risk.

When analysing the role of creativity in the innovation process, it is worth investigating more closely the nature of that creativity. One element which helps to give a practical definition to the concept is provided by Gertrud Höhler, for example, in her description of the creative person:

> Creative people handle knowledge and experience in a particularly efficient manner: they select flexibly between important and unimportant inventories of experience. In this way, they have experience at their disposal which best fits with the situation currently being encountered.

This description provides us with interesting advice regarding how to handle creative people within companies, in particular, the fact that they

need room to innovate, something which is all too often missing in rigid hierarchies. Höhler summarises thus:

> Creativity is the most expensive raw material of the future, an environmentally sustainable material which is unlimited in its usefulness to people, and one whose extraction is vital for the survival of western cultures.[10]

In attempting to sketch the picture of the top manager who is optimally prepared and suited to make creative decisions concerning innovation, one can easily run the risk of drafting an idealised image of a superhuman being who does not exist and, thank goodness, perhaps, cannot exist. Of course, the CEO is expected to be creative in the context of his or her strategic and integrative tasks, to have a feeling for innovations and their prospects in the market.

Room for Free Exchange of Ideas and Opinions

Above all, however, today's CEO is expected to provide colleagues with the necessary space which they need to be able to develop their own creativity. This may possibly lead to higher demands being placed on the CEO's personal skills than have been required for the development of his or her own creativity. It is certain that creativity will not develop among employees if they are forced into predetermined slots in a rigid organisation. Creative space is forged primarily via the structural and values-based framework conditions which the company establishes. Creating such space is often the simplest part of the exercise, since this framework can perhaps be established by more flexible working times, by relaxing the dress code, and more generally by removing clichéd, inherited business attitudes.

The real challenge for top management, however, particularly for the large and often fossilised businesses, lies in creating fruitful ground for the free exchange of ideas and opinions. That means not immediately 'dismissing' ideas which at first sight appear wide of the mark or sound confusing, but allowing such ideas and the discussion of them even when they may possibly be an irritant to the person at the top. This liberalness can generate a fruitful corporate culture; free thinking is very

much more important than the acceptance of trainers or T-shirts instead of a collar and tie, since ultimately these are only superficial signs of the freedom of thought which prevails within the company. If it comes to it, tyrants can also wear trainers. However, increasing numbers of progressive companies are taking account of such trends by adopting the 'dress down Friday' approach. Employees are particularly appreciative of this, if they normally have to dress in a formal manner for customer or client meetings. Yet we are already seeing signs of the reverse trend: the founders and employees of the company eBay.com, where there is no strict dress code most days, have decided to have an 'official Friday' where everyone comes to work in a shirt and tie, and trainers are banned. Freedom takes many different forms.

Releasing Creativity

A product development process which secures sustainable growth because it supports innovations which are fit for market must satisfy some fundamental requirements which are simultaneously core elements in a comprehensive programme for energising an enterprise.

Innovation management must move away from the monitoring function and towards releasing creativity. Whereas the test benches of the traditional development process were primarily concerned with eliminating ideas which were less good, today the primary objective must be to support good ideas.

Moving away from the 'market success' and towards long-term customer satisfaction is the second lesson of the new approach to innovation management.

Frequently, time and resources are expended on looking for a 'market success' which can take the hurdles of the internal company approvals procedures, but perhaps then no longer accords with the rapidly changing requirements of the market by the time that it is finally ready for launch. By contrast, what is needed are flexible, customer-driven processes which do not prolong the critical time-to-market factor.

The only possibility of releasing creativity within an entire organisation lies in supporting individual creativity. On the other hand, there is only one way to align product development with customer require-

ments, and that is by ensuring the involvement in the product development process of everyone familiar with those customer requirements. They must work efficiently together in groups which are formed on a cross-functional basis. Intelligent and creative employees identify themselves with their tasks in such project teams far more strongly than with the fairly uninspiring ideal of being a 'small cog in a large mechanism', fulfiling its function come what may – an outmoded concept which no longer squares with the self-image and the individuality of the 'adult citizen at work'.

In the new model of innovation, creativity is equally in demand in both the development area and the commercial process itself. Technological concepts are no longer categorised as promising on the basis of a top-down selection procedure, but on the basis that they are selected for commercial development by business people with a view to the demands of the market and the customers.

Under this arrangement, one management task with high priority remains the new orientation of marketing activities to take account of the great complexity of innovations in the area of technologies and products; this relates to the marketing of innovations, and to the development of innovative marketing concepts and methods which are required due to the presence of the Internet. The customer interfaces must be redefined and reshaped. Reorientation of marketing within the company must also contribute to improving customer orientation. The necessary integration of processes in marketing, sales, and research and development can also include putting in place a new responsibility for the market introduction of new products, namely the post of a budget-holding market development manager, who can be a vital factor in successful risk management.

CHAPTER 3

The New CEO Agenda

3.1 Perfect Balance – Stakeholder Value Versus Shareholder Value

Businesses operate in the emerging knowledge society in mature, largely saturated markets where innovations are the only means of giving new stimuli and generating additional growth. The conditions of globalisation and digitisation, understood in this instance as the basis of global networking, result in clearly expanded opportunities for one's own business activities on the plus side, while on the down side they result in heightened competition in formerly customary and often protected own markets, a consequence which is both painful and inevitable. Growth and the ability to compete can only be achieved by management with a new comprehensive, strategic vision of circumstances. Given the conditions for economic activity in Germany at the start of the 21st century, I would again emphasise the need for this strategic paradigm, which is aimed at achieving lasting success, to include, as an essential component, a more person-centred manner of viewing and managing the business. At issue here is stakeholder value, not simply a one-sided consideration of shareholder value. Only where stakeholder value is carefully balanced in the equation can an effort be made to do justice to the people factor as a success factor.

Admittedly, the stakeholder value philosophy includes the notion that company managements can only succeed in achieving a balanced consideration of all interest groups if each of these groups is temperate in its demands, if they do not upset or even destroy the desired balance

by lack of moderation. Moderation cannot be demanded as a virtue applying one-sidedly to the trade unions. The system is similarly unbalanced by one-sided pressure on prices and suppliers' terms and conditions (the so-called Lopez effect referred to earlier).

The first part of the following quotation from Wendelin Wiedeking has already been cited in the preceding chapter. It seems to me to be sufficiently important to be repeated – albeit in full – here in the context of stakeholder value:

> The only thing which counts is the ability of the company to move forward into the future. And you can only secure the future by enthusing employees and management alongside shareholders in pursuit of the common objective. By contrast, anyone who makes shareholder value alone the guideline for his or her actions cannot provide any security for the future. A high dividend payout which is achieved at the expense of a reduction in the development budget and in expenditure on training is a short-term pleasure – including, indeed especially, for the shareholder.[26]

Dr Wiedeking made this plea for the balance of interests to his shareholders – and they backed him. In making this appeal, incidentally, Wiedeking is also in solid agreement with the latest refinement and supplementary interpretations of the notion of shareholder value by its 'inventor'.

Misunderstandings and errors in developing the notion in practical terms have caused Alfred Rappaport, who was the first to formulate the notion of shareholder value, to make significant corrective additions to his idea: in his view, the mutual dependence of owners and other groups with a claim on the business requires them to commit themselves as a partnership to increase value, and also to see to it that the process of distributing that value is just. Creating values is something which Rappaport views as a long-term task, and he laments the fact that managements are driven by false principles of remuneration into adopting a short-term mentality which can only harm the business. As Rappaport puts it: 'The conviction to hold fast to investments which add value regardless of initial scepticism on the part of the share markets stands in the best tradition of shareholder value management.'[27] The 'father of shareholder value' sees the market and the relationship with

the customer as the key to increasing value: 'Where there is no value for the customer, there is no value for the owner either.' Rolf-Ernst Breuer, the former head of Deutsche Bank and present Chairman of its Board of Directors, has applied the same thinking to evaluating mergers. He sees them as being successful only if they ultimately bring some benefit to the customer.

Guided by Long-term Thinking

In the opinion of many top managers in German businesses, a management strategy which places long-term aspects before short-term maximisation of turnover and profit, with priority being given to long-term thinking, the pursuit of a clear vision and continuity of staff is one of the essential preconditions for sustained entrepreneurial success. That is one of the conclusions based on the results of a study jointly developed by Booz Allen Hamilton with two personnel consultancy companies in Germany and the USA. The aim of the study was to trace those criteria which give rise to sustained success lasting over many years. This enduring success was measured using the criterion of the increase in company value and based on stock market data, taking a ten-year period of study into account in order to neutralise the effects of speculation and short-term phenomena.

The study only considered those companies where securities had been quoted on the stock exchange for at least ten years, and where at least ten per cent of shares were in portfolio investments (free float). The size criteria were set at a minimum of DM1 billion turnover for industrial businesses, a balance sheet figure of DM10 billion for banks, and gross income of over DM4 billion for insurance companies. An additional filter applied in making the selection was that the increase in value had to be above the overall average in at least five of the ten years studied. This produced a ranking which generated a Top 20 for Germany and the USA respectively. Finally, from these Top-20 lists, candidates were selected for interview in order to identify the reasons for their continuing corporate success, using a comprehensive set of questions.

The interviews revealed that a second typical management behaviour correlated with long-term thinking: the corporate managers in the

German Top 20 have a definite focus on their stakeholders. They view the share trading price not least as a result of communication. Using permanent and transparent measurement of the results of all parts of the company and a strategy of continuous improvement, they secure lasting increases in value for all stakeholders. They know that long-term shareholder value can only be achieved on the basis of satisfied and motivated employees, customers and suppliers – in other words, of all stakeholders. Companies which have enjoyed lasting success – Siemens with its 150-year company history being an outstanding example of this – create their strength which lasts over generations from a policy which operates in that area of conflict between stakeholder value (understood as a long-term guideline to balance out diverging interests) and the necessary dynamism without which a future cannot be secured.

To some extent, in Germany, there is still a vague understanding of the concept of shareholder value, even in economic circles and after years of intensive discussion. Frequently, it appears that inadequate knowledge of the methodology is the reason for this incomplete understanding, which can naturally easily lead to misunderstandings. There can be no other explanation when the chairman of the supervisory board of a major company states in a management magazine, 'When viewed in terms of shareholder value, long-term projects often seem questionable', or when 'criticism' is voiced from the employee side that shareholder value is a 'cover for rationalisation and the loss of jobs'.

Methods with a Sound Basis in Terms of Company Economics

People should not seek to simplify things to such an extent. The reality is that the shareholder value method, as interpreted today by Rappaport himself, is based on sound concepts applicable to company economics such as the capital asset pricing model or the concept of weighted average costs of capital as well as on the estimate of final value.

Value-oriented corporate management and stakeholder value do not represent a contradiction in terms. This is something which even someone as highly placed as Jürgen Krumnow, at that time board member at Deutsche Bank, has made clear. Value-oriented corporate management is not conducted at the expense of stakeholders; rather, it

is impossible to maximise shareholder value in a lasting fashion if customers are offered poor products, employees are paid poor wages and the demands of the social partners are ignored. A strong company:

- Has strong shares with high stock market value, and thus high market capitalisation;

- Can satisfy customer demands for quality, speed of service and good price/performance;

- Can offer employees appropriate financial rewards, provide them with attractive opportunities for promotion, guarantee relative job security (the more successful the company, the more secure the job) and invest in their initial and continuing training with a view to the future;

- Can form an attractive area for sales and co-operation for suppliers and partners of the extended enterprise.

In short, it can do justice to the interests of all stakeholders in a well-balanced fashion.

With regard to shareholder value, the role of institutional investors in the circle of international shareholders dealing in globally active companies is repeatedly cast in a critical light. In assessing shareholder value from the viewpoint of these largely American professional investors, some noteworthy decisions are reached which should surprise only the apologists in the internal discussion about economic justice in the German context. Hans Konradin Herdt has described the issue from a perspective which makes a clear differentiation:

> The vision of the World plc sets high standards. At this level, corporations are engaged in global competition and the more international its shareholder base, the more pressing the invitations from institutional investors with their analysts to the infamous barbecue parties, in order to subject the figures and prospects for the companies and their management boards to a personal grilling, so to speak. Anyone who gets enraged about this fails to acknowledge that the institutional investors generally manage funds and pension funds which pay for the pensions of wide groups of employees. And the fact

that the Federal Republic of Germany, despite all the advance rhetoric, has still not succeeded in securing a lasting stimulus to its economy through the pension funds and similar instruments for making private pension provision is nothing but a testament to its lack of attractiveness and certainly no argument against such institutions abroad, who do not seek shareholder value for some nameless major capitalists, but for their clientele of regular workers. Seen in this light, the term shareholder culture acquires a new meaning.[5]

There can be no doubt that internationalisation is also leading to a more differentiated attitude towards the issue of shareholder value, and one which takes account of the socio-political aspects. On the other hand, the consensus thinking of the post-war period in Germany has become deeply ingrained at management level, even if it is called into question today in the face of the pressure to achieve competitiveness at the global level. Meanwhile, there is no doubt that progressive thinking in the aspects relating to shareholder value, without any acknowledgement of the principle of stakeholder value, cannot lead to lasting success.

3.2 Management with The People Factor – Leadership and Communications

Sober watchers of the corporate scene confirm that whether a company is successful or goes under – which may happen within an alarmingly short period of time – depends crucially on the man or woman at the top, regardless of whether it is a large, small or medium-sized business. This highest level of management, where responsibility and the power to take decisions are concentrated, must also be the source of impetus for the creation of a management team which is pulling on a single rope, and operating as a unit with regard to employees and towards customers and suppliers. Selecting managers who are able to operate in teams, from whom such an 'ideal team' can be fashioned, either by bringing them on in-house or by finding them in the open market, demands a lot of experience, knowledge of people and sensitivity – or what Rupert Lay terms 'life knowledge' – and is one of the most important tasks of top management.

The Leader of the Future

If taking the people factor into account is defined as a key precondition for long-lasting company success, then the question arises as to the qualities which the top manager and his or her system must possess in order that not merely lip service is paid to the people factor in the company's management principles, but it is something which is lived and is one of the measures by which his actions are determined. This question about the leader of the future was also put in September 1999 to Helmut Maucher, the godfather to the Nestlé group. Maucher's reply encapsulated the vast wealth of his life knowledge:

> For that, you first have to have all the personal qualities which have already been needed over the past thousand years: personality, responsibility, intelligence. The thing which will increasingly be needed in future breaks down into two components: first courage, nerves and composure, and second an ability to communicate both internally and externally.[28]

Alfred Herrhausen, the Deutsche Bank CEO assassinated by terrorists on 30 November 1989, stated his belief in the nature of the manager succinctly and memorably: 'You must say what you think, do what you say, and be what you do.'

The courage to take decisions and the desire for promotion at all stages of one's career were named by most of the 212 top managers surveyed by Heidrick & Struggles, Müldner & Partner as the most important success factors on their path to the top of corporate management, alongside a good education and training. An analytical mind is required, but so is the ability to present ideas verbally in a convincing manner. The ability to manage is not a team challenge:

> It is a challenge for the individual. In difficult times, the manager must be able to give clear instructions. In day to day business, however, the manager does well to talk with his employees and to learn from them, since increasingly he is dealing with highly qualified knowledge workers who are indispensable for the future of the company.[23]

The manager who wants to be successful in a networked and knowledge-based world must talk with his or her people and be able to

get on with them. To bring this back to the language of the manager, they must bring with them a high degree of social competence. To do this, they must have as wide a perspective on things as possible, a breadth of vision which is not limited to specific aspects of the company or even simply to technical issues relating to finance, but one which goes far beyond this to incorporate cultural aspects. The manager will also distinguish him- or herself above all by recognising and understanding the highly differentiated characteristics of different people, being aware of their needs, and taking into consideration their networking and their dependencies in the social mesh of the company. Equally, he or she needs to have a sense of policy contexts, in particular the socio-political contexts. Overall, this requires a broad range of fundamental knowledge.

It is precisely in a networked company, with its often widely different parts, that the ability of the top manager to integrate and his or her communicative abilities face their greatest challenge. The top manager is expected to represent and communicate the common objectives in a convincing manner. The entrepreneur working in a company at the start of the new millennium must expect to be an integrator to a considerable degree. The management team is no longer a separate caste. Without social competence, the top manager will not be able to overcome this challenge. In a largely emancipated world, leadership no longer means issuing commands or instructions, but means having the power to convince. This requires personality, a presence, and maybe even charisma. Social competence is reliant on the vehicle of communication.

Social Competence is a Challenge for the Management Personality

The American psychologist Daniel Goleman introduced a new concept into the vocabulary of management with his catchy phrase 'emotional intelligence'. Booz Allen Hamilton, which for decades has been familiar with the importance of the soft factors and has a wealth of practically based implementation experience, prefers to use the term 'social competence'. The ability of managers to motivate, understand intuitively the viewpoint of their counterpart and be able to get on with

many different types of people, the qualities of teamwork, composure and discipline in dealing with spontaneous emotions – these are all criteria which make up the people factor.

Like all apparently pithy phrases, the concept of 'social competence' runs the risk of being used as nothing more than a fashionable buzz word whose substance is no longer considered. How does one acquire social competence, which must go far beyond the ability to handle the works council skilfully, even in critical situations? How does it mark out the manager? And does it perhaps require some institutional provision to instil it, perhaps like a voluntary year devoted to social competence? In the USA, there has been such a route to acquiring social competence for a long time, and in a manner which is fully accepted by society. It results in bonus credits for courses of study and training, and can make it easier to progress to responsible positions. Of course, this is only one of many possible opportunities for gathering experiences in social contexts outside the world of stringent, success-oriented career planning. This can also mean experiences acquired in the course of working with other people in a social context, irrespective of whether this is with a charitable organisation, St John Ambulance, or as a volunteer with the fire brigade; we are talking of experiences which one necessarily gains in overcoming problems when interacting in a social context with people of different cultural backgrounds and/or other social classes, in other words experiences of a completely different order to those relating purely to the narrow world of professional life.

Anyone who looks at the densely packed curricula of the élite universities and business schools, which take people to exam level after eight semesters, and the requirements of businesses following these periods of study, naturally finds himself asking where the necessary time to acquire these experiences in social contexts can be found. Today's university serves and operates far more as a place of goal-directed career preparation than as a place of learning in the sense of the ideals propounded by the German scholar and statesman, Wilhelm von Humbold. However, there are many things which go to suggest that the manager who aspires to achieve top management positions must necessarily take this time out to gather experiences which cut across his or her chosen career, which can be referred to as life experiences. This trains people in a kind of learning which is indispensable and which

generally makes it easier to overcome people-related problems in one's later professional life.

The experience of how to get on with other people is not only acquired in the narrow field of social commitment, but can equally and similarly intensively be acquired through sport or cultural activity, for example as an amateur stage performer – even though this may initially seem a little odd. However, when acting you have to give of yourself, and transport yourself into different characters who are perhaps wholly contrary to one's own nature. You have to be able to take direction, to think and act as part of a team. If one reads the memoirs of the Dutch entrepreneur Frits Philips as he remembers his parts on the student stage at the Technical University in Delft,[29] then it quickly becomes apparent that this is one way in which the ability to get on with others is instilled. Ultimately, the acquisition of social competence is also a process of self-education, putting one's own 'importance' into perspective, conscious insight that one's own infallibility is a myth, and recognising that some criticism is more justified than one might like to admit.

Taking such considerations into account, the challenge for our education and training systems can be described using the classic 'T-model'. The horizontal line represents the necessary breadth of education and the vertical line represents depth, the single specialist area in which, as in the past, it is necessary to acquire in-depth knowledge and experience in order to be successful. And it is doubtless correct to seek to develop this knowledge rapidly rather than extending one's period of study open-endedly. But, to develop the image further, it will become equally important that the top bar of the 'T' has sufficient breadth to go beyond the subject area, even if as a result the depth which can be achieved in the chosen specialist area is less than before.

Both Breadth and Depth of Training

Even in the German university system, which for a long time prided itself on the general studies course, there are initiatives aimed at re-establishing the breadth of education. Organised as a 'laboratory for developments in university education' and launched with high expect-

ations, the University of Erfurt, founded in 1999, offers basic general studies which comprise 20 per cent of all student courses. It supplements the social sciences and humanities courses at the university. Its first Vice-Chancellor, Professor Peter Glotz – who has since become a chair-holder in St Gallen – explains:

> Students graduate from us with a Bachelor's degree in applied knowledge. They then have a basis of knowledge in the social sciences and humanities on which they can build throughout their lives. But these students know that graduation does not mean an end to learning – they go into jobs and come back to the university at some later stage.[30]

Private universities, like the European business school, with their obligatory semesters spent abroad in English- and French-speaking regions, offer educational, cultural and personal experiences which doubtless extend the horizons of the students at the same time as providing them with a period of residential study abroad.

Through breadth of education, a more comprehensive understanding is developed of other relationships, including non-economic relationships. Furthermore, when one considers that globally operating companies are increasingly active in the Asia/Pacific region, where completely different cultural mind-sets and living and working conditions are found, the need for managers to have a breadth of knowledge very quickly comes to the fore. It can be critically important for business success to preserve old cultural values, respect them and deploy them successfully; for example to be aware of and take into consideration in daily managerial life the role which careful development of business relationships over a longer period of time plays in Asia. Managers who have thought long and hard about the issue of education and training and have moved away from the well-worn paths plead for an education which is humanistic in character, in which people learn to think over longer time-frames with a horizon of 15–20 years. People should still be efficient, but should also acquire an insight into their actions and the consequences of their actions.

Broadly based education and training and in-depth expert knowledge of a specialist area are indispensable preconditions for leadership without the traditional 'power of command'. To this can be added the need for life-

long learning. Even learned management techniques – and this is something which Rupert Lay acknowledged at an early stage – do not necessarily remain useful throughout one's life. In respect of the young, well-informed, self-aware, creative and innovative Internet generation, this view immediately proves insightful.

Visions – Opportunities and Risks

The ability to develop visions for the future of the company ranks highly among the wide-ranging spectrum of requirements of the CEO at the outset of the third millennium. Naturally, this cannot mean visions which form in some space unrelated to purpose, as it were, but visions which are directed practically towards a particular purpose, such as:

- Elaborating, formulating and developing the central task for the business, or in other words, repeatedly adapting to the dynamically changing environment;

- Defining the core competences in the product and/or services area, and working determinedly to drive forward their development;

- Elaborating and expanding on a clear differentiation of corporate services.

It is part of the essence of these visions that they are always concerned not with bringing about static situations, but dynamic processes where there can be no standing still.

On the other hand, there are examples to indicate that what seem at first sight to be major and fascinating visions can mean major risks for a company, and ones which it may perhaps no longer be possible to control. This is how many people view Edzard Reuter's vision of an 'integrated technology group' at AEG which swallowed up billions of marks, or the visions of oil trading profits by Heinz Schimmelbusch – as examples of the dangers of holding on too doggedly to visions once they have been developed, while their relevance to the real world altered. It is probable that it will never to be possible to completely avoid such risks. The most important corrective in such instances is

having the personal strength to be able to recognise mistakes which have been made at an early stage and to correct them. That requires a considerable measure of courage and a readiness to listen, and also the ability to be open, in order to be able to pick up on outside stimuli. The danger lies in putting up barriers, in pressing ahead with tunnel vision, simply because one does not want to see or admit to mistakes to oneself or anyone else. Incidentally, this applies equally to top managers and politicians! The readiness to recognise mistakes and learn from them is extremely important.

There is an evident connection between the inability to have self-critical insights and the rigid hierarchical structures which are passed down. The person who has climbed to the higher levels in the hierarchy finds it increasingly difficult to admit to mistakes and acknowledge these to colleagues who are always seen as competitors. By contrast, Jürgen Schrempp had the courage to be open about the misguided investment in Fokker, and ultimately took the mistake made by a whole team on 'his shoulders'. Companies and the public have respected his courage.

Continuity of Binding Values and Culture

Continuity in company management is without doubt an essential prerequisite for the sustainable development of businesses. However, internationally conducted surveys by Booz Allen Hamilton show that CEOs and managing directors remain in their leadership positions for ever shorter periods (see section 3.3). In the USA, this trend is currently even more marked than in Europe, as a result of the compulsion to show short-term success from quarter to quarter.

Since corporate continuity can no longer be maintained in the person of the CEO, it becomes all the more important to develop a continuity of binding values and clearly defined objectives. Naturally, this task is highly complex in the extended enterprise. Continuity of values and objectives can only then be achieved if the CEOs not only optimise returns and shareholder value for the short term in the limited time-frame which remains available to them under today's conditions, but also engage intensively with values as an essential element for long-term

success. Only in this way can a culture develop which will endure beyond the time in office of the CEO and, ideally, will remain as a living entity relatively independent of the people in the company. Considered from the viewpoint of values-based leadership, person-centred management is concentrated on the core abilities of the company which originate in the body of employees, the management and the organisation. These – somewhat intangible – core abilities are located in the heads and hearts of the people who deliver the service, which includes suppliers, dealers, importers, service providers and partners. The whole network has a common value orientation at its core. Person-centred management aims at maintaining and extending values which are created by people for people in the extended enterprise. In this area, more should be demanded of the supervisory board. It is far easier to demand all this than to realise it in the day-to-day existence of the corporation.

The corporate culture defines in broad terms how the network of intangible core abilities can provide the necessary services most successfully, and what the practical development goals look like. This is apparent above all from the behaviour of people within the company and in the relations with partners: concepts such as quality awareness and social awareness, flexibility, praise/recognition, openness to ideas and a sense of 'us' describe positive patterns of behaviour; concepts such as bureaucracy, injustice, arrogance, a know-all manner and taking decisions on someone else's behalf all reflect negative patterns of behaviour. The greatest gift which a corporate culture can have can be transcribed in the words justice, fairness and independence. There is no fixed definition of the term 'culture' itself. Justice is a constituent part of every democracy and every democratically rooted organisation. Fairness means having consideration for those weaker than oneself, refusing to take advantage of others and recognising those people or things which are better. Independence is the basis of freedom in personal development, in forming and expressing one's own opinions, and the acceptance of responsibility. Laws, rules and regulations are not by definition just, fair, capable of generating space for creativity and supportive of development, but they are always a firm part of a stable culture which sustains values. The CEO secures trust in the common objective, first through his or her own conduct, and second through perceptible corrective measures in the event of inappropriate conduct.

Engaging with a corporate culture – improving it, making it something which lasts – demands a clear and considered setting of priorities within the necessary tasks, given the short period in office and the daily pressure of time, and at the same time requires insight into the need to secure success for the long term. A broadly based education and training which aims to prepare for the role of the generalist manager, an extensive range of experience, a sense of cultural values and the ability to communicate are extraordinarily helpful components in the intellectual and mental range of abilities for the top manager, equipping him or her for the task. Regarding the extent of education and training for the top manager of the future, Richard Sennett, a communications academic, voiced the following opinion, which has significant policy ramifications:

> I am firmly convinced that in future there will be bank directors who have previously studied archaeology. The important thing is to equip people with key qualifications: the ability to communicate, handling complexity, languages, mastery over the computer. But I do not believe that the multifarious demands of the digital society and of the jobs in this society can be taught at university. These have to be learned on the job.[35]

Communicate Openly and Motivate

The ability to communicate is a shorthand phrase for a further aspect of people-centred company management which impacts on management decisions in more than just a peripheral manner. Here I am referring to the acceleration in the flow of events which has already been mentioned several times in this book, the speed with which changes take place in the corporate environment and which forces the company into similarly rapid, and as far as possible proactive decisions or rapid reactions. The problems which arise from this for management are presented in such a way that the difficulties of managing 'fast' companies appear to be bigger than those of managing a 'slow' company. However, rapid decisions can only be taken with no loss of care if the information relevant to the decision is complete, comprehensibly prepared and appears rapidly on the desk, or, more accurately, on the computer screen. Know-

ledge management and competence networks prove themselves to be indispensable services in such a context.

Returning to communication, this has already been described as being as irreplaceable for the corporate culture and the working atmosphere as it is for the implementation of changes. This applies above all in the critical phases of mergers, takeovers and other forms of incorporation, in other words in those phases where it is vital to win or to maintain confidence. Communication has also gained in importance because company managements must take their employees and the people operating in the environment around the company particularly seriously in a context where decentralised structures and networks are the norm – far more seriously than was the case in the age of a centralised command economy, which is not all that long in the past in the case of (the former East) Germany. The level of the demands made by employees has changed markedly. Companies are badly advised if they think that these demands can be ignored. Open communication must take place today even if it is a painful process. Of course, that is often more difficult than simply pushing things 'under the carpet'. On the other hand, those affected can cope with a remarkable amount if they are told openly 'how things are', what has to happen and will happen, and if they have the feeling that they are not being palmed off with half-truths. Naturally, the best situation is when they can also be given some prospects for their own future at the same time.

Practitioners know that this is often not possible in the relatively short time of a change or merger process or in crisis situations, under the applicable conditions found in German industrial law. For reasons of legal compulsion, the company management is repeatedly required to follow certain procedures with regard to information, even in the most critical situations. With regard to employees and public, the management is even obligated by law to maintain silence when it is apparent that the joint management–employee economic committee, the works council and the staff are not complying with the legal regulations regarding confidentiality. They hope (and are proved right, incidentally) that by providing this initial information to the media they will secure advantages in handling public opinion and will simultaneously force the company onto the defensive in its dealings with the media by forcing it to provide justifications. The larger the company,

the less it can afford to depart from the path of clear value orientation and strict adherence to principles and the letter of the law. If the element of leadership of public opinion, which is highly important in crisis communications, is lost and passes to the attacking party in the dispute as a result, then this is painful but often unavoidable in the case of disputes under industrial law.

How bitter the experiences relating to the issue of crisis management and crisis PR can be, even when the company is completely innocent, is something experienced by ex-Formula One driver Niki Lauda when a Lauda Air Boeing 767 crashed in Thailand in 1991: 'You are completely on the defensive, because the others – the press, the experts, the competition – supposedly know more than you do' (and, one should add, manage to give a lead to public opinion as a result). However, at that time Lauda also discovered the key to successfully coming through the crisis:

> Fortunately, we accelerated our internal information flow to the point where we were quickly better informed than all the others. This meant that we were rapidly able to take the sting out of the press speculation.[31]

Communication is an indispensable management tool, irrespective of the specific crisis situation. The issue can be reduced to a simple formula: if you are talking with one another, then at least there is a personal element involved, however slight – or at least there is the opportunity to make contact on that level. If talking with one another is taken literally, and time is taken to have a face-to-face discussion, then another significant effect comes into play, which can be summarised in the short phrase 'proximity destroys prejudice'. In other words, entre-preneurs who want to break down internal and external prejudices must not engage in putting up barriers. They must seek to achieve proximity with others.

As a globally operating business which practises the daily balancing act between two continents, histories and cultures, DaimlerChrysler has defined communication as a key tool for leadership and motivation – particularly in terms of wanting not just to address the mass of its 420,000 employees in five continents, but to actually reach them. The company uses its own internal television programme in seven languages

to reach 452 locations, each with over 100 employees, via 5000 TV sets. The daily 20-minute broadcast comprises current news and features. In 260 locations, there are additional local text pages accessed via TV.

At DaimlerChrysler, as at other progressive companies, people are fully aware that leadership must make use of modern media as multipliers. However, people are also aware that even the best appearance on the TV screen cannot replace personal closeness. One must be clear about the fact that communication is the vehicle, and not a substitute, for thinking and messages. It is important that there is consistency of thinking in lasting values, and that the message is credible. The decisive feature for the lasting impact of the manager – the term success is deliberately avoided here – remains the status accorded to the people factor in his or her world view and maintained regardless of all the obstacles of everyday corporate life. Of course, this is a challenging standard. And I know there are many, indeed too many, examples to show that these obstacles are sometimes stronger … in these instances, even the most well-constructed communications concept cannot help, since it lacks the core of credibility.

3.3 Accepted Models: Consistency of Actions

If one asks older top managers who have weathered many storms how they assess the chances of a manager succeeding in making the people factor one of the measures by which they operate, then not uncommonly the immediate response is a gentle – and depending on the temperament of the person – even mocking – smile, as a fitting response to the supposed dreamer asking the question. Other interviewees, who are more disposed to offer a considered response, say that this and only this is the right approach, if it is bound up with a definite rigour in going about it. Of course, owners and supervisory boards also expect proof from these managers that their approach is the better one for the long term. However, one should also be clear that it can be difficult for these managers to see through this approach in a consistent manner, because they are constantly having to weigh up the requirements of shareholder value and the demands of employees, customers and suppliers. On the other hand, these managers know that shareholder

value can only be realised if one has motivated and committed staff. 'The people factor will always play a leading role', says Dr Karlheinz Bozem, today a partner at Booz Allen Hamilton, and formerly deputy board chairman for the energy company EnBW.[32] When asking what constitutes this people factor, one receives a wide range of responses, from justice through impartiality to fairness, without which partnership-like management in modern, flexible organisations with flat hierarchies is not possible.

This and many other characteristics have entered into the model of values-oriented management. In the knowledge society, which is presently starting to develop out of the information society, value-oriented management must react in an intelligent and responsible manner to the diverse and profound changes which are taking place with great speed both structurally and in the relations between employees and companies. In essence, this type of management must satisfy only a few simple-sounding requirements: it must allow the individuals in the company room to develop as individuals. It must provide them with and guarantee them the same rights and the same possibilities. Encouraging performance and efficiency is among its foremost tasks, but it must also ensure that order is maintained and take vigorous action to preserve order. Without procrastination, it must dismiss those who are unwilling to perform. And it must take account of its responsibility towards the community and for the community. Of course, these simple-sounding things constitute a highly challenging programme. With regard to the specifics of the knowledge society, management is faced with the task of creating a culture which promotes the open exchange of knowledge and rewards the conduct of those employees who participate actively in this new openness. Requesting openness from employees presupposes an open rather than a hierarchical management. Permanent communication, recognition of problems and abilities and commitment at all levels are elements of values-oriented management which are just as important as delegation of responsibility and the constant aspiration to improve abilities and competences, as can be optimally achieved in competence networks (see section 3.7). If one successfully strengthens the self-confidence of people in a company, then it becomes significantly easier to achieve acceptance of the constant change to which businesses as living organisms are subjected,

in much the same way as constant change affects the positions, functions and responsibilities of individuals in project-orientated organisations. If one has self-confidence, one can look with far greater equanimity at a changing professional future.

Far-sighted managers can only agree with Dr Klaus Mattern, Vice President and member of the Board of Directors of Booz Allen Hamilton, that one of the most pleasant duties of the manager consists in being successful by making others successful. Success is a motivator. Motivation increases the readiness to perform and the performance itself. The old maxim, that nothing succeeds like success, remains as true today as ever. The task for the manager is to light the initial fuse.

The Jesuit priest Professor Rupert Lay, who is referred to in this book in several places as a figure providing intellectual and moral direction, describes the necessary breadth of knowledge of the top manager using the fitting term 'life knowledge', by which he means the ability to recognise what human life means for oneself and others. Lay was once asked: 'If you could put together the ideal manager, what elements would you include?' Lay's answer is classic in its simplicity:

> Firstly I would expect him to be an honest person. That, for example, he does not confuse objective truth with subjective certainties, that he knows what he is talking about, that he is not, for example, just pushing set phrases around. Second, that he can get on with people. Specialist knowledge and experiential knowledge will in the long term increasingly come down to us via the Internet. It is therefore important that a manager has life knowledge, that he knows the importance of human life for himself and for other people. And then third, of course, that he has an understanding of ethics, and lastly that he is in a position to implement the decisions which the team takes.[33]

Statements such as these, particularly at the present time, are a great encouragement, when it appears evident that not only some top managers, but even the political leadership are losing their sense of the ethical context.

Growth has Priority in the CEO Agenda

There are a series of elements which repeatedly occur on the current agendas for the new CEOs, irrespective of the size of the company or its sector. The percentages shown in the following list indicate the frequency with which each element appears on the agenda of the companies interviewed:

Generating growth	30 per cent
Refining/improving the business portfolio	26 per cent
Improving financial performance capability	22 per cent
Communication in the organisation	22 per cent
Change of organisational structure	19 per cent
Change in company structure	19 per cent
Reducing costs	15 per cent

Continuity in company management is, as already demonstrated, a vital prerequisite for the sustained development of companies. This contrasts with the fact that the 'half-life' of CEOs has dramatically reduced over the past ten years. The tendency is for the CEO of today to have less time to cope with his or her package of tasks, which is by no means reproduced here in full, because on an internationally assessed average he or she will only remain in this top post for around seven years – in Europe, and particularly in Germany, this may perhaps extend (a little) further. Of these seven years, one to two years are lost to the handover phase of working one's way into the company, and at the end a similar period of time is devoted to the handover to the successor. This means that a top manager spends around a quarter of his or her time as a CEO in handover phases. (Considered in the global context, the half-life of the CEO is becoming even shorter!) Handovers of this kind are almost always difficult, sometimes even awkward, especially since the newly appointed CEO in most cases brings no experience at that level to the post, since one only takes on such a job once in a career or once in a lifetime. And the bigger the job, the fewer the number of people operating at the same level who can be asked questions and with whom one can talk openly. Loneliness is the price of life at the top. And one must pay particular attention to ensuring that one does not oneself contribute to becoming isolated and thus ultimately lose one's social competence.

The Half-life of the CEO is Getting Shorter and being a Role Model is More Difficult

This means that there is also less time available to develop and behave as a role model. As a result, company managers must concentrate even more on demonstrating consistency in their actions.

Another phrase comes to mind in connection with this: leaders need followers. It is characteristic of rigidly fixed structures that management functions are very often designated from above rather than being developed in dialogue with the employees concerned. Imagine that employees in a department in a traditional German company were today asked to choose their departmental manager. They are asked to nominate the best and most person-centred individual from among their own ranks, with the nomination going to the employee who can make most things happen and do good things for the company, someone from whom one can learn and who can be trusted to give leadership in the role. The result would often be significantly different from the top-down choice made by management. Naturally, the employee chosen from below would have the better followers. And experience shows that it is not only the most agreeable and the weakest characters who are chosen. There may be some truth in the view that employees may possibly rate the empathy factor higher than the competence factor. But as a rule, however, one will find – and in my experience it has indeed been the case – that employees attach great importance to the competence of the future manager. In future, there will be a need for both these processes – that is, top down and bottom up. Being people-aware consists not least in not underestimating the ability of colleagues to make correct judgements and in respecting that judgement. The important feeling that one is being treated justly, perhaps even fairly, is most often generated by such an approach. Here too, it is the case that without a well-developed ability to communicate there can be no fully developed factor of empathy or competence.

Communication also includes the nonverbal elements of communication – all top managers would agree on this: facial expressions, gestures, and one's behaviour in general. Old status symbols are proving more and more to be obstacles in the way of attaining that new openness which is being argued for here. Of course, there are closed doors for

important, confidential discussions, where staff issues are discussed, for example. But otherwise the open door to the manager's office is strongly symbolic – and a model for middle management, which sees its old status as being increasingly under threat since Intranets have speeded up the information flow across all levels and thus simultaneously accelerated the transition to flat hierarchies.

There has been a similar transformation in the role of the PA. Whereas for decades the PA had served as a gatekeeper, an impassable obstacle on the route to the manager, and whereas his or her own importance within the company was augmented by screening off the manager (not uncommonly against the manager's own wishes) and increasing the manager's importance by his or her very inaccessibility, today's PAs see their role as that of the intelligent, helpful assistant, who regulates but does not obstruct access to the manager – and equipped with the useful ability to perform that function at all times with a smile. Space in which to operate is created for the manager by guarding his or her back against organisational trivialities.

Together with the gatekeeper in the anteroom, other status symbols have long since become obsolete. The liveried chauffeur permanently on call, who instead of spending his evenings at home passes the time in smoke-filled chauffeurs' rooms among his fellow drivers, all waiting for the end of a meeting, a meal, a reception – in most companies, this figure has long been consigned to history. And where he has not been lost to a better vision of what matters, he has all the more clearly been dispensed with due to the pressure of costs.

That is enough of the specifics and the detailed considerations: openness is demonstrated in modern companies in diverse and quite unpretentious ways. It gives clear and unmistakable signals to employees.

There is a clear relationship between fair treatment and personal space in which to operate creatively within the company on the one hand, and the readiness to perform on the other. People who feel good about themselves can deliver better performance. This means that management figures should pay more attention to the mind-set of employees. When verifying her mode of expression test, Elisabeth Noelle-Neumann found: 'the people with a lot of subjective freedom to take decisions in the workplace were always happier, healthier, more active, and more friendly in a social context'.[34]

3.4 A Vital Community: Values, Culture, Customers

The extremely divergent, almost paradoxical development has already become apparent: while society – and here I am looking particularly at Germany – can agree less and less on common values, companies are being presented with a role which is difficult to define and yet one which they must perform, recalling their lived values to serve in effect as a centre of values for all employees, offering a point of stability in an environment which is devoid of orientation. Long-standing centres of values are fragmenting more and more, irrespective of their often major traditions. In the extreme instance, one is left with the lone worker at the computer screen, who in future is ever more often isolated from his colleagues and working at home in front of his monitor, lost to friends and family, for whom the company perhaps remains the final tangible centre of values and orientation. For the management, this means that beyond pay and opportunities for promotion, a wider social function must be acknowledged which can no longer be managed without the people factor.

A Lived Canon of Values is The Basis of Success

> But how can long-term objectives be pursued if one is living under the framework of an economy which is wholly aligned with the short-term? How can loyalty and obligations be maintained in institutions which are constantly breaking apart or repeatedly being restructured? How do we determine what in us is of lasting value, if we live in an impatient society which concentrates solely on the immediate moment?

asks Richard Sennett in his reflections on the flexible individual, which are particularly marked by the American experience.[35] The managers in the companies of the 21st century cannot ignore such questions, even if they are in the grip of a short-term mentality which is present in Germany in a distinctively different manner from the USA. They are still required to provide answers to these questions which address the people factor. The basis of these answers can only be a lived canon of

values which is taken on board by people who are distinguished by that same ethical standard which they apply to their own decisions and to their relationships with the people in the company.

An equally simple and directly illuminating maxim for values-based management has been formulated by Helmut Maucher: 'Do nothing which could not be reported the next day in the newspapers.'[28] In stating this, he has simultaneously described the role of the public – or, more precisely, of published opinion – as an ever-present and relentless court of judgement. That holds true for companies just as much as for politicians and all institutions in the social sphere.

The issue of values-based management demands expression in practical terms. Like other soft factors, it shares the inherent risk of being so much well-sounding waffle. So what can/must values look like where they are not simply to be the subject of quality talk, but are to be the qualities by which companies live and work? If one takes the commonly mentioned values and sets them opposite practical measures over which top management can exert direct influence, this generates a short and clearly comprehensible list:

Notion of value	Practical 'application to'
Creating trust	for example in management, in the strategy, the objectives, the immediate supervisors, in statements from the board about job security, in the competence of management
Guaranteeing the value of the individual	for example in the event of redundancies, in instances of harassment at work, management style
Ensuring appropriate conduct	for example towards subordinates, in dealings with suppliers, in networks, confidentiality
Exercising fairness	for example in the appraisal process, in correcting faulty outcomes, in addressing inappropriate conduct

Recognising performance	for example for successes by individuals or teams, in appraisal, in the bonus
Rewarding courage	for example for taking on the role of devil's advocate, for taking a lead role as a change agent, for unusual ideas and suggestions in discussion rounds
Creating acceptance	for example for unpopular measures, for new staff when incorporating them into the team, for speed, for change

Communicating these value messages is more successful and more rapid the more clearly they are reinforced with practical, comprehensible actions by top management. Because the acceptance of values always involves processes which run over a longer period of time, critical importance attaches to the continuity and consistency of the communication, which is aimed at generating a lasting and profound impact. Last, it involves such problematic objectives as:

■ Generating understanding

■ Securing commitment

■ Developing self-confidence

■ Acceptance of change.

Taking the view of Herbert Demel, President of VW in Brazil, one can see the task of top management as being 'development workers for human potential'. This is an extraordinarily rewarding task, since effectively this potential is lying dormant, simply waiting to be aroused, brought to the surface and allowed to develop. Fundamentally, the individual takes a delight in performance, and gains satisfaction from work which has been successfully accomplished. This feeling is in no way restricted to the justifiable pride of the carpenter who has produced a well-made piece of furniture, but applies to all sectors where an individual's performance can be perceived, recognised and acknowledged. This point cannot be emphasised enough, after a long period when

performance was equated with the pressure to perform and viewed in negative terms, as the result of ideological preconceptions.

The CEO thus creates the necessary framework for the realisation of values within the company. The most important values for the success of the company are determined by people, markets and customers. The driving force for these values is competition. Only those things which are the best in the long term create assets (shareholder value), employment (social value), customer satisfaction (customer value) and prosperity (economic value). But the most important values relating to people in modern organisations form the basis of all successful businesses: respect for the individual, fairness, courage, justice, recognition, generosity, openness, space in which the individual can develop.

Creating an atmosphere of willingness to perform, and a climate in which people want to be successful and are rewarded for their successes, is a person-centred endeavour in the best sense of the term. Values-based management creates good prospects of achieving this.

Former Intel Chairman Andy Grove knows that pay and incentives, including stock options, are necessary to keep good people, but he also knows:

> What really attracts top managers is the prospect of belonging to a winning team. The economy is no different from sport in that respect: good teams never have problems in attracting good players.[23]

In my experience, tensions arising from unsatisfactory incentive structures derive above all from the fact that employees are not rewarded in accordance with their expectations. But where these structures are fair, that is, transparent and just in their arrangements, the teams are happy and motivated, and get on very well with one another on a personal level.

Young people are growing up quite naturally into this new, open world under the influence of globalisation. They travel in their early years, gather experience of getting on with people of other races and cultures at an early stage, and no longer experience the linguistic difficulties which presented a problem to people even as recently as a generation ago. And they want to take decisions, even where these are associated with risks. Their intensive familiarisation with information

and communications technologies begins in school; here they enter a world which will become familiar to them, and an indispensable part of their professional world tomorrow. For them, it will be a matter of course that they will apply for jobs without regard for country boundaries, that they will aspire to international careers. Thus globally active businesses will of necessity become multicultural structures in which employees with different mother tongues, different experiences and different ethnic and cultural backgrounds work together productively. Their integration presents new challenges to management – and not just in the personnel section. Perfect knowledge of foreign languages, which goes beyond vocabulary to include a familiarity with the other, different cultures, is the key to productive collaboration, frequently supported nowadays by a common language within the company group, and often by intensive preparation for the future work environment in terms of the country and its people, set in a different religious, historical, cultural world of thought, customs and habits. The economy is belatedly following the model of the diplomats' school.

A Simple Principle: Reward What Can Be Influenced

In the climate of the new understanding of self between employer and employee, incentive systems which are not solely concerned with key financial ratios acquire greater importance. Whether an incentive system works to motivate and proves useful depends on whether the person being evaluated can him- or herself influence the factors being measured. The performances of employees must be measured by those parameters which they themselves can actually influence and affect.

Many incentive systems include factors over which the employee has no influence, over which he or she can make no decisions even when in a management post, with the result that the employee's performance cannot be accurately measured. The decisive feature of such a system is to find a balance between those things which the individual can influence directly and the performance as a team over which he or she can have an influence through joint target-setting and teamwork. In Germany, many incentive systems are based on hierarchical structures and measure targets over which the individual can have almost no influ-

ence. At best, such systems are useful in areas such as marketing and sales, where clear attainment targets can be set. In the upper tiers of management, however, the assessment criteria become more problematic and more vague. Incentive systems under which employees receive high praise without making a contribution which matches up to it should be avoided. They are perceived to be unfair.

Above all, corporate values must prove their worth in change processes, which include company takeovers and mergers, as mentioned earlier. The core message always aims (more so in periods of change) to make changes understandable and acceptable as something normal, to reduce the fear of dynamic change, and simultaneously make apparent in a convincing manner that the shared values do not change. The better a company succeeds in securing identification with the objectives and ideas of value held by the company on the part of its employees, the easier it will be for the company to gain acceptance for change processes.

At first sight, this relationship may seem to bring together two things which stand apart: in the impressive architecture of American company head offices, one finds an expression of the readiness of companies to acknowledge social roles. Even relatively small companies equip themselves with impressive head offices, because on the one hand they impress clients, but on the other hand they want to provide employees with opportunities for identification on an emotional level (pride in 'his' or 'her' company). Naturally, in voicing such considerations one must immediately expect the objection that these are simply the 'cathedrals of capitalism', that much of it is merely architecture intended to impress or to assert authority. Certainly, this cannot be denied. But it is also true that in this way identification with the company is enhanced, that positive feelings relating to a place with a sense of 'professional belonging' can develop, enabling one to cope better with the 'no-man's land' of the Internet, which particularly in Germany is often vigorously charged with being a cold and unwelcoming environment. According to Baldur Kirchner:

> Identification is the result of the ability to form emotional attachments. Becoming enthused, inspired or even animated by a person, a thing or an idea presupposes the ability to form identifications.[46]

In the leading industrial nations there are industrial buildings which merit being termed icons of identification. One of their special characteristics is that their effects outlive the clients who erected them. No one in New York would dream of renaming the PanAm building in everyday parlance, even though PanAm planes have not flown for a long time.

Companies are increasingly gaining a better understanding of the importance of corporate identity, and use it consistently to put their employees in a positive frame of mind. They therefore see themselves as faced with the task of including more and more all-embracing issues in their spectrum of values, such as cultural activities, in a broad sense. Without a corporate commitment to culture – to the benefit of its own employees as well as the advantage of the local/regional audience – in many places the cultural sphere would be significantly poorer, given the dire state of public funding. However, such a lessening of provision would reduce precisely that attractiveness of location expected by the demanding high performers of the economy. Therefore this means that further diversified incentive systems must be applied and the factors which can be directly influenced must be measured, and these must react to differences.

Culture as a Factor for Location

Cornelis Bossers, the former Chairman of the Board at Philips Germany, has clearly defined the reciprocal effects of cultural sponsorship and the quality of location:

> For economic businesses with a constantly rising proportion of widely educated and demanding employees, the cultural components of urban living, and the urban lifestyle itself, are a location-influencing factor, which has acquired and continues to merit importance to the same degree that traditional factors influencing location, by virtue of its geographical position, economic significance or for technical reasons (e.g. infrastructure), have lessened in importance. It reflects a new socio-economic reality if entrepreneurial thinking and actions are not satisfied with passively taking note of the existing circumstances with regard to education and culture in the location, but see a joint responsibility and an opportunity to create some-

thing in these areas as well ... It is a courageously embraced objective of such efforts to strengthen subtly the power of the metropolis to attract economically active people through its new qualities in terms of education and culture.[36]

Thus an ever stronger local/regional responsibility for values is being created.

The aim of a large number of change processes which are currently underway or being pushed in businesses is to achieve greater proximity to customers, to make customer orientation a primary component of the corporate culture. Making the customer the centre of entrepreneurial thinking and daily action is one of the key success factors – independent of the size of the company and the sectors, regions and cultures. Progressive companies have a very simple credo on this issue: I only have an advantage over the competition if I am quicker and know more about my customer than my competitor. Niki Lauda used the example of his own Lauda Air to describe how customer orientation and customer service can be critical factors for the company's survival:

> I pursued a new concept. At Lauda Air, we offer a sensible meal and sensible service in safe aircraft. In our business, that is really the only competitive advantage which I can offer. The planes come from Boeing or Airbus. The routes to the frequent flier destinations are practically identical. So the only thing I can improve is the service to customers.[31]

Optimal customer satisfaction is achieved if the customer becomes, so to speak, a (willing) advertiser for the company. Customer orientation of this quality can only be achieved and established on a lasting basis through the role model lived by management. Customer orientation begins in the management board. Top managers should personally know and keep up contacts with that 20 per cent of customers from whom the company realises 80 per cent of its turnover.

Recognising and knowing customer desires is more difficult than ever because they have become increasingly differentiated since the experienced customer has come of age. With the growth in customer independence, it has become markedly more difficult to predict purchasing behaviour. Programmes to develop customer commitment are now fash-

ionable. The belief in price promotions in the consumer area as a means to achieve customer commitment appears unshakeable – although the benefit of the programmes depends to a large extent on whether these are embedded in a profound corporate culture of customer orientation. A fundamentally customer-centric approach pays off in measurable terms for companies. According to recent studies, such companies are on average 60 per cent more profitable than companies who believe that they can operate without above-average efforts in the area of customer commitment. Even with all the scepticism proffered about quantitative statements for qualitative patterns of behaviour, it is nevertheless apparent that there is a clear correlation between the degree of customer-centricity and business success. Price policy, product quality, customer service and motivation of employees are the areas of action where consistent customer orientation must be effective.

Customer orientation must also play a role in situations where management might be distracted, at least temporarily, namely during company mergers and acquisitions. Rolf-Ernst Breuer, former CEO at Deutsche Bank, remarked at an event focusing on investment banking that company mergers and takeovers are sensible only if the customer also has a sense of added value. Only then would customers bring greater turnover to the new entity, and shareholders and the share price would benefit from the merger. Breuer confirms that customer orientation, pursued seriously, is a key element in the strategic alignment of companies and corporate culture.

Sponsorship of cultural or sports events can, if combined with company-specific events and opportunities for meetings, create more than just exclusive experiences. It can also provide a suitable social context for this kind of customer orientation at the highest level; for example sports sponsorship can generate impressive successes across a wide range of customers, which also proves that the soft factors elicit tangible market effects.

At the start of the new millennium, management guru John Naisbitt envisaged a new megatrend, which aims to achieve customer proximity through specific product design: high touch – technology which touches, in the literal sense (that is, having an impact on the emotional state of the user). Naisbitt believes that high touch satisfies a completely new trend in demand, namely customer interest in high tech in a design which radiates

user-friendliness. He believes that what matters is how we experience high tech in our daily life, and argues that this requires a critical consumer who is aware of the role which modern technology plays in his or her life. Naisbitt's credo is that high tech must be in harmony with human needs. There is solid evidence to demonstrate that user-friendliness in having the high touch look is more than the fertile material of a bestselling guru. Since 1995, Siemens AG has been operating a special test laboratory for user-friendliness. Heidi Krömker, Departmental Manager at Siemens with responsibility for this test laboratory, comments that usability will in future be the only way to sell products, and 'our goal is to optimise customer benefit and customer satisfaction'.[57]

3.5 The Thrust of Motivation – Post-merger Integration

Mergers and acquisitions have quickly become an essential element of modern company strategies and growth strategies. Regardless of the huge increase in company mergers, the results of current research show that less than half the merged/taken-over companies were successful – measured by the actual business results in comparable companies. Despite the increase in experience, the success rate is not improving. As in the past, mergers are frequently challenges and risky strategic decisions, where the people factor at all levels often plays a key role. These insights are taken from a study of best deals, in which the corporate consultancy Booz Allen Hamilton examined 117 important mergers to find out the causes of their success or failure.

Before every merger, it is vitally important that supervisory boards, managements and shareholders are fully aware of both the opportunities and expected risks. Before this risky path is embarked upon, it is important to weigh up carefully whether the merger is the best strategic option and represents optimal use of capital – measured against traditional investment performance; and this should take place against the background of the major complexities bound up with a merger. Among the findings of the study, it was discovered that there was no direct relationship between the market or share value paid for a company (which leads afterwards to large write-downs of goodwill) and the success of the merger. Businesses which paid a high additional price (such as Vodafone

Airtouch for Mannesmann) were generally clear about the fact that the merger was only a step along the way to realising their long-term goal, according to the findings of the study. Incidentally, neither the examination of relative size of the merging businesses nor the question as to whether mergers took place in associated or different industries produced noteworthy findings with regard to the success of the merger. In 1997 Booz Allen Hamilton interviewed 35 companies worldwide with relevant experience as part of a study 'Making Acquisition Work – Capturing the Value of the Deal', and discussed with them the influence of a wide range of tactics on the merger's success or failure. The most important finding was that the most successful companies combined an effective strategic formulation of their vision, and of the objectives of the merger or takeover which derived from these, with practical planning of the phase before the companies are merged and careful integration following the merger. All three components taken together are decisive for success.

'Speed, speed, speed' was Jürgen Schrempp's phrase when looking to drive forward the process of integrating Daimler and Chrysler. The first hundred days are critical, as we read in the headlines. The London School of Economics proved in a study that mergers frequently fail because there is too long a period of hesitation when implementing a merger even following a decision to merge. At the time of the merger of Sandoz and Ciba Geigy to form Novartis, three insights were formed by Daniel Vasella, the first Chairman of the Board for the new company group, which largely agree with those of Jürgen Schrempp and the London School of Economics:

- a merger should be completed as quickly as possible;

- the specified schedule should be observed without fail;

- all conflicts between the partners to the merger must be openly discussed.

And finally, the new company should set itself objectives which are as ambitious as possible, so that employees do not get sidetracked into discussions over trivial matters.

It is part of the insights of the managers and company advisers involved that the companies which best handled and came through

takeovers and mergers were the ones which already had the relevant experience. In this regard, Cisco is an ideal company to cite as an example, since the rapid growth of Cisco was accelerated by an unbroken chain of company takeovers. Within six years, around 40 companies were taken over, at a cost of over 17 billion dollars, and successfully integrated under a 'Single Enterprise Program'.

When Cisco acquires a company, it is not only because of its current products, but also because of the people who it takes over, since Cisco then acquires the next generation of expertise and competence and, therefore, products. Cisco CEO Chambers comments:

> If you pay between 500,000 and three million dollars per employee and all you are doing is buying the current research and the current market share, then you are making a terrible investment. Under the average acquisition, 40–80 per cent of top management and the critical engineers leave the company within two years. If you include this measure, then most acquisitions go wrong.[56]

At Cisco, by contrast, the rate of haemorrhage in recent years has been only 6 per cent. Cisco sees two keys to success: intensive preparation in order to select the right company using reliable criteria, and the introduction of an effective and comprehensible integration process once the deal has been concluded. A major aim of this process is to make clear to the new employees that they are welcome in the new company.

Is There a Clash of Cultures or Interests?

Hans Konradin Herdt suspects that:

> Even more strongly than with the acquisition of foreign companies or the establishment of foreign subsidiaries, a liaison between companies which in formal terms are of equal status sees a clash of the most widely diverging interests and cultures, both in the highest circle of management and also lower down, right through to the level of production and sales. I suspect that often the interests lie much further apart than the cultures, and sometimes the two are confused with one another.[47]

Albrecht Schmidt, the HypoVereinsbank chairman with an outstanding track record of experience in mergers, knows what he is talking about when he declares: 'A merger demands courage. But above all, it requires enormous discipline.'[47]

The management task for the first hundred days, as a matter of absolute necessity, is to make positive use of the disquiet generated in the course of the merger, which develops out of uncertainty about the future. Employees expect changes in this situation, they worry and become fearful. Because they want clarity about their future, change processes should not be prolonged over many months. Decisions are accepted so much better the faster they are taken and more openly they are communicated. Acceptance levels are naturally higher if those concerned can recognise clear prospects and opportunities for themselves. The newly created larger company needs continuity as soon as possible, a rapid return to normality. And that can only mean centring attention on the customer, and achieving added value at the new, higher level.

When mergers take place, it is repeatedly evident that serious differences in corporate cultures can cause mergers to fail even when the economic and rational preconditions are entirely unaltered. It is all too easy for visions to turn into serious loss-making ventures as a result of unbridgeable cultural differences, which in the worst instance can mean the end of the company's own freedom to act and be creative.

Where mergers or takeovers occur across national or linguistic borders, there are additional problems which are often underestimated. Specific national, even regional cultures have their own developed characteristics. Where conflicting cultural specificities come up against one another, they can form the core of the failure of a corporate merger. Different cultures require a high degree of attention by management and sensitive handling of the respective 'other side'. DaimlerChrysler is a clear example of the various aspects of this issue.

Often, companies which are ready to merge discover too late that they do not suit one another. Thorough and completely open consultations between small, properly constituted representative teams from both companies can help to avoid many problems in advance of a merger (while maintaining the strictest confidentiality), by examining critically whether what the management boards would like to bring together will actually marry up. Uncritical enthusiasm would be a poor

counsellor during this process. Differences must be discussed behind closed doors, without reservations, and examined to see whether they can be bridged. Sweeping these differences under the carpet could ultimately be dangerous, for they will not stay hidden. They will come to light when it is too late. On the economic side of a merger process, it goes without saying that all the facts must be analysed critically. As a minimum, a similar level of care is appropriate for the much more problematic process of bringing people together who have different ways of thinking and behaving.

Wolfgang Bernhardt, Honorary Professor of Corporate Management at Leipzig University, has described the cultural aspect of mergers and takeovers in graphic terms:

> A company is more than a framework of figures, and an employee more than a 'number'. Anyone who takes from a company its history, its sense of self, its culture, its name, its connection with a specific landscape and environment – in short, those things which make it feel comfortable, without justifying this action convincingly and comprehensibly and/or without being able to replace this with something equally or similarly able to sustain the company will hardly achieve success in the medium and long term, and will pay the price of that, if measured against the opportunities.[37]

In the final analysis, it is the execution and implementation which determine the success or failure of mergers. As Professor Bernhardt puts it: 'Here it is decided whether an industrial dream develops as a reality or a nightmare; and that depends primarily on the people at all levels in the business or joint venture.' Bernhardt's experience has shown that 'mergers can lead on into a great future, but they do not get there automatically and are no insurance against the injustices of everyday entrepreneurial life'.

The Internet Supports the e-Merger Process

Alongside the central task of bringing people together, every merger also brings a set of problems which are barely less complicated and cause distress not just to the responsible IT managers: the transform-

ation of the financial and operating information, which is almost always structured differently, into a common standard format in order to provide a reliable common basis for taking decisions. Consultancy experts talk of the e-Merger process in this context, describing a process which runs in parallel with the merger and which in ideal circumstances is already completed by the time the actual merger of the companies is effected. (The Internet technology provides decisive assistance in this, even if the e-Merger application deviates considerably from the normal use of the Web.) The following stages mark out the e-Merger process: at the start of the merger, each of the two companies has unchanged access to its own data and, in addition, to some data belonging to the other company; at the end of the merger, all data must be available to the new combined company. For each business unit in the new organisation, detailed and standardised financial and operating information must be unrestrictedly available from day one of the approved and realised merger onwards. In other words, mixed teams from both companies must introduce the process sketched out here at an early point, so that there can be access as soon as possible to a well-introduced reporting system. In this form of collaboration, starting at an early stage, there are also good opportunities to get over the 'gulf' which naturally separates the two staff groups at the outset. Positive experiences gained through working in such integration teams need to be discussed in both companies.

Combining companies – whether on the basis of takeovers/buy-outs or mergers (including the so-called mergers of equals, where in the end it is always the case that one side is 'somewhat more equal' than the other) – has certainly resulted in serious changes in management as well as for the employees, in the majority of cases. The company managements are put under pressure, they must realise those synergies which they generously calculated to make the deal appetising to their supervisory boards. Merger plans often include the separation of parts of companies and thus also of employees at the different levels – perhaps because they no longer fit in with the new common strategic focus, perhaps because their sale is necessary for a rapid decrease in the mountain of debt which has piled up, or perhaps because subsidiaries and participations must be disposed of on grounds of cartel law. The merger of VEBA and VIAG is a concrete example for both forms of separating

off companies, but also for the planned merger of subsidiaries in which, as a result, there was a surfeit of management positions.

The question as to how much space exists in such processes for the people factor – in the sense of fairness and honesty – is one to which there are not many convincing answers, although I am sure all top managers would agree that even the necessary and painful redundancies for managers, who generally live without the protection of employment legislation, can and must be arranged respectfully and maintaining the dignity of the person involved. In that process, manner and conduct are at least as important as money.

Rationality On its Own is Not Sufficient

From many personal conversations with my father, Dr Wolfgang R. Habbel, the former Chairman of the Board at Audi AG, I recall comments and suggestions which sit very well with this assertion. There can be no doubt that the manner in which a process is undertaken and the personal conduct of the manager are of great importance, particularly when it comes to difficult decisions which may have a major impact on employees, their personal work context and their corporate environment. In such circumstances, cold logic on its own is of no use. Whether one is talking about or with the persons affected or whether the conversation is about the change itself – in each instance, the people factor can be allowed to feed in. Even where the conversation is about the need to dismiss a manager in the near future, it is possible to find a sensitive and fair form of words and approach which is better for the person concerned, but also for the company itself. The effect and the subsequent reverberations are certainly more positive than in response to a cold and purely rational procedure. This is also the hour for the personal courage of the top manager to come into play. He or she should not shrink from conducting these difficult discussions him- or herself. The top manager can and should not leave such discussions to the head of personnel or others. The manager concerned has a right to hear the final word from the person at the top if he or she is being told he or she must leave the company and why. If one applies this standard, then it is apparent that even at higher management levels courage is not a quality shared by all.

In transformation situations, the unexpected departure of managers causes a great deal of unrest at top management level and among second- and third-tier managers – and in some cases in the media – particularly if the people involved are respected and widely known board members/managing directors. There can be many reasons for such an eventuality. Often, those leaving are not satisfied with their positions and prospects in the new corporate federation. And sometimes it is down to the 'headhunters', who sense their opportunity, during mergers and turbulent times, to offer frustrated managers glittering opportunities with the competition (which in uncertain times can sound very attractive indeed).

Following the takeover of the American banking house Bankers Trust (BT) by Deutsche Bank, there were a considerable number of personnel changes at BT and switches to direct competitor companies, which was painful for the acquiring company, despite the fact that Deutsche Bank had made available a special reserve of over 400 million dollars in the course of the takeover, to be used for special payments in the first three years following the takeover to those employees whose collaboration was of particular interest to the bank for the future. On the other hand, at an early stage plans were tabled for the removal of 5500 jobs, mainly in New York and London. That accelerated the process of positions disappearing – even if the people leaving were not always the ones who would have been let go in any case. The series of departures began with high-quality managers in share and bond trading, continued through the tier of managing directors and peaked with the resignation of CEO Frank Newman, who had negotiated the sale of BT under conditions which were highly advantageous to him. He was followed by the Head of Finance Richard H. Daniel, the number two in the BT hierarchy. Lastly, a team of fund managers also switched to the opposition (Merrill Lynch).

The development of new common structures for DaimlerChrysler and the integration of the two businesses on either side of the Atlantic was described as exemplary by experts at an early stage. However, it quickly became apparent that Daimler was dominating the process, notwithstanding all the fine words about a 'merger of equals'. It may perhaps be for that reason that even DaimlerChrysler was not spared the early departure of high-status managers such as board member Thomas

E. Stallkamp and Co-chairman Bob Eaton during the transatlantic merger, together with the associated publicity.

Andy Grove, as former chairman of a knowledge-based company, takes a very sober view of the set of post-merger problems: 'If we buy up a company and the most important knowledge workers make off, then we have lost out already.' From this, he concludes that 'the loyalty of our employees has a considerably higher value than in the past'.[23] Companies must therefore do a lot more to retain these employees following a merger. The cost, in hard currency, has already been made clear from the example of the takeover of Bankers Trust by Deutsche Bank. Money alone is not enough to achieve this. The soft factors must be right, and break-ups as a result of cultural differences must be avoided.

Loyalty Seen in a New Light

Among the worst side-effects of takeovers and mergers is the systematic and focused removal of the first and even second tiers of management of the 'subordinated' company or of managers in the direct sphere of influence of the former chairman of the board of that company; such action is neither explicable nor justifiable in rational terms. Their only 'crime'? Loyalty. Under this procedure, which can be observed not only during takeovers and mergers but also when there is a change to a new chairman of the board who is predisposed to take such a course, there is a destruction of resources and reserves of knowledge and experience which defies all sense, but which curiously is rarely criticised in the financial press.

Seen from the perspective of corporate culture and confidence in management, the hostile takeover is the least desirable option, because it is the most disadvantageous starting point for sound and people-centred integration of those taken over into the victorious company – even if the supporters of the Anglo-American share culture repeatedly swear that the hostile takeover is not a sin. This is where one of the fine dividing lines between shareholder and stakeholder value lies.

Generally, as already stated, acquisitions serve to buy turnover volumes and market share, in other words scale, strength in the market,

and growth. It may very well be the case that sometimes (and perhaps even not uncommonly) what is at stake is corporate self-awareness. In many instances it can be a rewarding strategic objective to use acquisitions to secure new employees with knowledge and creativity who will help to guarantee tomorrow's growth. Integrating these employees, giving them the sense that they are not simply being 'swallowed up', but that they are being offered new opportunities and new possibilities – including for personal development – in the bigger corporate grouping, is a task requiring a considerable degree of sensitivity and character. Acquiring companies and then subsequently losing the people who embody their performance and expertise through a lack of sensitivity is probably the worst kind of business deal imaginable.

The more valuable the contribution of the individual for the future of the new corporate grouping, the more secure his or her position. To put this in a more sobering light: it is not past performance and service which counts. Major companies do not take gratitude as one of the categories which frame their thinking. Accordingly, there is greater emphasis placed on the ability of the manager, the researcher and the developer to orient themselves to the requirements of the future – developing new competences which are in demand, using knowledge which is constantly being acquired, the challenge for the individual, just as it is for the company as a whole. Accordingly, the learning company is not some abstract ideal, but a core element to secure the company's continued survival. The new understanding of relations and responsibilities between companies and employees, which is the subject of the next section, can be useful in overcoming critical transformation situations for the individual. In place of sentiments which no longer appear in tune with the times, it proposes greater autonomy and independence of the trained employee with up-to-date knowledge, for whom a job for life in the same company is no longer a prospect to which he or she aspires.

3.6 Fairness with Responsibility: Accepting Mistakes, Allowing Risk

The radical nature and pace of all this change bring about developments which always affect the individuals in companies first. And perhaps

no other change in the world of business is more marked than that in the relationships between the companies and their employees, and between the employees themselves. Values and standards of conduct, which have endured since the start of industrialisation over two hundred years ago with relatively modest changes, are now being called fundamentally into question in the economy of the third millennium.

Accepting responsibility for employees was a central entrepreneurial task in the industrial economy (and even earlier too, in the times of feudal rule). It is not surprising that it has led, under the conditions of the period concerned, to very different and by no means always dignifying forms of welfare support, as we understand the concept today. For a long time, the ideal form of this support was taken to be securing a job for life – even into the 1950s and 60s, this was rewarded with the Federal Services Cross (equivalent to the OBE in Britain), awarded by the Chairman of the Regional Council, and a gold watch from the employer. Pierre Coureil, formerly Vice-President of Booz Allen Hamilton in Paris, has described the traditional corporate model graphically using a practical example:

> Around 40 years ago, when the well-known top manager Charles Handy began work at Royal Dutch Shell, his employer could relocate him and his family worldwide as often as it wanted, under the terms of his contract. If he wanted to have a career, Charles was to set no boundaries to his commitment and loyalty. In exchange for that, he knew that Shell would ensure that it satisfied his needs and those of his family, being aware of its responsibilities. At that time, employers offered job security, a stable working environment and a staged increase in responsibility and pay in exchange for absolute loyalty and good performance.[38]

In the era of global competition and the frightening acceleration of all change processes, this guarantee of employment has become impossible to fulfil – for the company, but also increasingly for the new-type employee, who has learned early on that he or she is responsible for him- or herself. This insight obliges one to acknowledge the necessity of redefining and reformulating the relationship between companies and employees.

Pierre Coureil describes the 'new ethical contract' which needs to be entered into in a credible manner as follows:

> The company undertakes to invest in the employee, so that the qualifications which he or she has in the employment market increase. In return, the employee is responsible for determining his or her career unhindered. It is his or her duty to add value to the company and to maintain his or her own value in the market. The employee and the company must *work together* to develop common competences which guarantee both the competitive ability of the company and the employability of the worker. Employees are, in the truest sense of the phrase, working with rather than for the company.[38]

Ensuring Employability

Naturally, here we are describing an ideal situation which is still often far removed from reality. On the other hand, this new thinking is increasingly finding a place in companies which are managed progressively. 'If our employees are employable worldwide, then we have acted responsibly' emphasises DaimlerChrysler CEO Jürgen Schrempp as he addresses this central fact of the new relationship between employees and companies. But even when faced with this fundamental change in the relationship with employees, developing a new form of loyalty on this new basis still has an unchanged – or even an increased – priority within the responsibilities of management; and this loyalty is also of far greater importance than in the past. The absolute preconditions for this are motivation, decent pay (I have deliberately chosen to use the 'old-fashioned' concept of decent), and the feeling that employees in critical situations are 'not left to face it alone'.

From the company's point of view, what Pierre Coureil has termed the new ethical contract must satisfy four objectives. This contract must make it possible for the company:

- To be attractive to the best-qualified workers (to represent a team of winners);

■ To motivate all staff in such a way that they exploit their full potential, and to provide them with a suitable environment in which to do so;

■ To develop competences continuously; and

■ To achieve a balance between the interests of all involved.

Only a modern company, in the best sense of the word, which has recognised the central importance of human capital will be able to satisfy the first of these four requirements. It must on the one hand offer its people working conditions under which creativity and calculated readiness to take risks can develop fully. On the other hand, it must protect its international competitive ability through a steady flow of innovations.

Studies by the World Bank suggest that a good two-thirds of the wealth of the rich countries is attributable to human capital. Only a sixth is attributable to physical capital and natural resources. In a study published in 1998, the OECD concludes that the economy in general suffers from underinvestment in human capital. In many countries, up to 50 per cent of those eligible to work are not capable of satisfying the demands of today's knowledge-oriented economy. These statements are based on practically based tests of skills, on an evaluation of the returns from training, measured by income, on research and development in the relevant country, and of course on an evaluation of education and training in schools. The results of the skills tests in twelve countries were classified into five assessment categories. Those who did not pass more than the two lowest levels would, according to the OECD, barely be capable of handling the demands of the new economy. A particularly striking detail is that this applies to 41.7 per cent of all people eligible for work in Germany. In the older age group, between 46 and 55 years, this proportion is at its highest. The risk of becoming unemployed is very high for those who have the least qualifications.

No company can increase its value, grow and remain competitive if employees are not motivated – including being motivated to constantly develop their own qualifications and competences. Pierre Coureil emphasises that companies need staff at all levels who can and want to go to the limits of their ability to perform. They must understand the objectives of the company in a comprehensive sense and be prepared to participate in determining the fate of the company:

Ultimately, it is their duty, under their sense of personal responsibility, to ensure the competitive ability of the company, since they possess a major part of the knowledge and the competences which make up the company's performance.[38]

Qualifications Determine the Value of the Company

This definition of the personally responsible employee simultaneously describes the fundamental change (and increase) in the importance of human capital for the company. Former Intel Chairman Andy Grove describes the change very vividly:

> The value of most companies no longer consists in the ownership of factory plant, but depends on the qualifications of its employees. Tomorrow's products are above all knowledge products ... If a production worker leaves the company, the tools and machines remain. A new worker can take over the duties without difficulty. If a microprocessor designer quits his job, he has got the tools in his head and simply walks away with them. That is a completely new situation.[23]

From this new vision of the role of the individual as a knowledge carrier and decision-maker, as a source of creativity, intuition, vision and innovation, there arises an almost forced reassessment of the value of knowledge, which is raised to the status of being the fourth, and possibly decisive, factor in production. Knowledge management is one means of minimising the risk of loss of knowledge sketched out by Andy Grove. The next section is devoted to this issue.

A key precondition for motivation and a readiness to perform is decent pay for employees. Decent means that one measures employee performance against fair, individual and objective target values. As one of the elements determining the success of its comprehensive performance management initiative, Booz Allen Hamilton defined a performance-related pay system at an early stage. Establishing suitable control values is an important precondition for objective assessment of an employee's performance, and for the associated pay rewards. These control values must, as already mentioned, be stripped clean of all

exogenous factors – those factors over which the person being assessed has no influence.

To demonstrate what is meant by this, let us take as an example an all-purpose bank typical of those found in Germany, with an extended branch network. Branch manager A runs a branch in the best suburban district of the city; his colleague B runs the branch in the densely populated working-class area. B can make all the efforts he likes, but he will never be able to achieve the number of customer deposit accounts with significant amounts of securities held by colleague A. However, when it comes to procurement loans and other small loans, and in terms of the number of savings accounts which generally contain modest sums, B clearly has the advantage. It will only be possible to assess the performances of the two branch managers in a serious manner if, for example, the different economic and demographic factors in the assessment are input into the process, to differentiate between them. The two colleagues, and with them all other colleagues at branch manager level, can only feel that the assessment of their relevant performance is just if their work is measured against those factors over which they can have some influence.

A thought-through performance management system facilitates close linking of pay to the results of the assessment system. In this way, the company management can recognise and appropriately reward outstanding individual and team performances. We have already discussed the fact that this reward need not only relate to money or other benefits with a monetary value, but for example may also include the opening up of opportunities for promotion and intangible benefits.

Thanks to performance assessment which is objective in its content, performance management also particularly opens up opportunities for self-development to the person being assessed, for under this system performance strengths and weaknesses are identified equally, and always on the basis of those factors which are relevant for the success of the company. Managers are thereby shown how they can make their area more successful; the company management can recognise the areas where fundamental changes and improvements are required.

Although the example given here is based on organisational forms which have been passed down over time and which are not likely to disappear that quickly, it is true to say that for employees in companies with

new forms of organisation the growing responsibility for defined parts of process chains will take the place of positions within the hierarchy.

Stronger Identification with Projects than with the Company

This also throws up new points relating to the issue of motivation. 'Identification with individual projects will be more important for motivation, in my view, than identification with the company as a whole', is how Professor Dr Frieder Meyer-Krahmer, Manager of the Fraunhofer Institute for Systems Technology and Research into Innovation describes the new role of employees and their greater responsibility for parts of process chains.[9]

It is precisely under the conditions of employee responsibility in new organisational forms with flat hierarchies and strong team orientation, with a changing composition of temporary project teams and against the background of the notion of personal responsibility that a finding made by Helmut Maucher is of major importance:

> In my experience, the selection of people is a hundred times more important than their training. If we get the wrong people in, then afterwards I can pump in millions in training and information, and the added value might be perhaps one per cent.[28]

For top managers, this defines that responsibility for people (which I have described as the original entrepreneurial challenge) in wholly practical terms.

A comparable decision-making situation arises over the market introduction of a new product or a new service. It takes personal courage to see that a product does not satisfy expectations and must be pulled from the market, while one can repeatedly use new marketing measures to build up new hopes, even if these come at a huge price and can all too easily prove to be illusions. On the other hand, completely new kinds of products need a very long time before they gain acceptance from consumers. Vacuum cleaners, dishwashers, video recorders – all were novelties which at the time of their launch had to overcome considerable reticence on the part of consumers before they could become major

market triumphs. It has long been forgotten that it took a considerable period of time before the first million black-and-white television sets were sold in Germany in the 1950s.

The Obstructive Chicken-and-egg Situation

New products require a particularly long period of time, with the chicken-and-egg problem coming into play – as for the television set, as just mentioned, which could only become a success when a suitable selection of programmes was available. Sometimes developers and marketers simply have false expectations of the needs of consumers and their priorities. The video recorder was marketed as a 'time shifting machine'. The idea behind it was that programmes could be watched at a different time. But then came the demand for pre-produced video cassettes, particularly those with content which the then still prudish public broadcasting channels were keeping from their audience. It was only when the selection of content on cassette had reached a suitable volume that the market for recorders 'stalled'. Ultimately, it was the availability of a sufficient range of pre-recorded cassettes which determined the outcome of the battle of the systems between Europe and Japan. The technically superior European system Video 2000 and Sony's Betamax finally fell to the power of the demand-led market.

A positive counter-example is the rapid and wide market launch of CD players and CDs. The inventors of the system, Philips and Sony, both owned major operations in the music industry and were able to drive forward the parallel introduction of hardware and content. Their power in the market was large enough in both areas to compel the competition to 'play along'. However, the rapid development of the Internet places even this success story in the shade.

These few examples show how difficult and how weighty the decisions are in the area of innovations and product launches. However, one thing holds good and true: managers must be allowed to make mistakes. Admittedly, mistakes due to a lack of insight and personal vanity lie beyond the necessary thresholds of tolerance, which can be recognised much more clearly if one has defined the threshold of risk well beforehand.

Limiting risks through market research is something which is repeatedly attempted, often with notable success. However, when it comes to a radically new product or design, surveys of buyers/customers quickly reveal their limitations, because the customer has no idea of such leaps in technology and lacks the imagination to embrace completely new designs. The expensive flop of the Ford Edsel marks one of the low points in the history of market research. The expenditure on market research for this car was greater than for any other car previously launched onto the market. In the end, though, the car made history only in the case studies of American business schools from Harvard to Stanford. A different but similarly expensive example is the magazine *Leute*. It is taken here as a representative example of many flops in the print media market. Media are extraordinarily complex products. If they are to be economic successes, they must gain acceptance not just from the envisaged target groups but also from those placing advertising. It is very difficult, perhaps even impossible, to ask future readers how they would imagine a new print medium which they would be prepared to buy or subscribe to. Demands are made of the creativity and the imaginative powers of consumers which they cannot possibly satisfy, even with the best will in the world. The publisher is lucky if it possesses an adequate number of editors and a compositor with this skill. It is only rarely that the publisher him- or herself is the top creative figure in the company, as is true of Dirk Mantey and his publishing house 'Milchstraße'. How much a new media product depends on a single creative thinker has been demonstrated above all in recent years by Helmut Markwort with *Focus*.

There is a significantly lesser risk with derivative products and spin-offs from existing print products. The highly successful group of publications around *Bild* – from *Auto Bild* to *Computer Bild* – is a positive example, similar to the more recent titles from Milchstraße and up to the Internet spin-off *Tomorrow*, which Burda then followed with *Focus Digital* and another interesting new business model. Platform concepts represent a further way of reducing risk, one which is pursued above all by the mass manufacturers of the automotive industry. So long as these are practised in a measured way, so that they do not lead to cannibalisation effects owing to too great a product similarity, they can make an interesting contribution to limiting risk because they help to minimise

development costs and bring alternative products which are fit for market onto the market quickly, thereby also reducing the critical success factor of time-to-market. However, companies in the top segment of the selection of automotive products take a rather more sceptical view of the platform strategy.

Introductions of new products are frequently still pursued with no attempt to guard against the risks involved, despite all such considerations. The almost unavoidable flops then lead to an increased unwillingness to take risk, which ultimately creates a climate which is hostile to innovation. Guarding sensibly against risk and the readiness to take risk therefore do not have to be mutually exclusive. On the contrary, they are two sides of the same coin. Computer-aided scenario techniques are useful in filtering out risks. They are suitable for including a large number of risk factors and elements of the risk impact chain in the calculations. It also enables a large number of options to be worked through quickly. It is also important that such calculations are constantly updated to adjust to changed internal and external circumstances.

If companies are managed in partnership, as is often the case with management consultancies, engineering consultancy companies and advertising agencies, then the risks to be run are shared among all partners. What is measured is the overall result. That allows the individual partners to cushion risks. At the same time, they are mutually answerable to one another as owners and therefore create the necessary transparency.

3.7 Continual Cell Division: Knowledge Management, Competence Networks

It is not the limited availability of raw materials, but the unlimited availability of knowledge which is the decisive resource in the competition for global markets: competitive conditions, customer requirements, technologies, markets change – more rapidly, more profoundly, more surprisingly than ever before.

This idea comes from Jürgen Schrempp, and was advanced at the 7th annual seminar of the Alfred Herrhausen Society for International Dialogue. A few years ago Betty Zucker, of the Gottlieb Duttweiler

Institute, put forward the idea that knowledge was the first raw material which increases as it is used. She believes that this fact impacts on management.

At a high level of abstraction, knowledge can be defined as an asset which reflects a (tacit or explicit) understanding of how something functions (process knowledge) or – to put it very generally – how the future will look (content knowledge). Of course, knowledge always has meaning. Fundamental insights into knowledge as a driving force in change were known to the classical philosophers: 'The only lasting thing is change', acknowledged Heraclitus of Ephesus around 2500 years ago. In the language of the present day, and in connection with our theme, the message is that the change all around us is knowledge-driven. But for a long time and even into the present, knowledge has been the preserve of the individual; when thinking in terms of the economy, industries or technologies, this knowledge is concentrated in individual researchers, technologists, managers. It was focused and still often focuses on a single patent which is perhaps pioneering in its impact. By contrast, innovations in the 21st century (and in recent decades) are frequently based on combinations of very complex knowledge structures and whole bundles of patents. Their association and linking increasingly take place in competence networks. In the past, knowledge was not perceived as an asset to the same extent as it is in the highly technologised, networked world of knowledge-driven industries in the Net economy, where the USA today still has a decided advantage over Continental Europe. There are reasons for this difference.

Acceptance and Use of The Internet Hindered by Europe's Fragmented Markets

Acceptance and use of the Internet by consumers and for business purposes have been relatively hindered up until now by Europe's fragmented markets, when compared to the state of development in the USA. Now business people and observers are anticipating positive development within the coming three years, first in the B2B area, and after that in the consumer area, as soon as markets and currencies are standardised. At the end of 1999, according to the German Economics

Institute, less than half of all companies in Germany were making use of the opportunities afforded by e-Commerce – and that despite the fact, according to the same source, that in 2000 goods and services totalling DM6.9 billion were traded via e-Commerce in Germany. SAP's Hasso Plattner envisages that in five years all businesses will be Internet companies because their success depends to a considerable extent on how far they succeed in becoming a component of the globally integrated value-added chains, with the help of the Internet. The study already referred to cites a series of reasons for Europe lagging behind in this area – from the lack of a common language through the high costs of telecommunications to a certain dislike of credit cards.

In Europe too, however, there are today already a large number of encouraging developments. The British government, for example, is according the issue of e-Commerce such importance that it has appointed a minister with special responsibility for electronic trade.

Among the far-reaching effects of the I-World will be the fact that it will bring about a new distribution of roles and functions in the economy, because, according to Klaus Wellershoff, Chief Economist for the major Swiss bank UBS, it is creating new markets 'which up until now only existed in the economics teaching books. Through the Net, we are approaching the perfect market.'[39] New additional functions and areas of activity are being developed, which must also be defined, for example that of the broker and the application deployer – that is to say, those people who discover, record and understand ideas, and those who are able to project and implement this understanding in terms of products, services and markets. They build the bridges between ideas, needs and distribution in the market. Microsoft CEO Bill Gates is perhaps the most fascinating example of this new broker function, and this is by no means on account of his billions of dollars, but thanks to the specific abilities which ultimately have resulted in these billions. The new brokers of the I-World are very typically knowledge workers – creative people thinking in an interdisciplinary manner and with the ability to associate knowledge from various sources intelligently to produce new knowledge at a higher level. It is only with careful, people-centred management that it will be possible to provide this new type of employee with a working atmosphere where they will feel comfortable, thanks to the significant freedom within which they can operate.

Alongside this new perception, companies have learned to understand the dangers inherent in knowledge of relevance to the company being concentrated in individual minds. Andy Grove highlighted the problem with his reference to the fact that a microprocessor developer simply takes his 'tools' with him if he quits his job, because he has got them in his head. With this example, Grove has also given a revealing justification of the need for knowledge management, which finds its most progressive expression in networked competence domains, to which the fourth part of this book is devoted in detail.

The courageous leap over the significant obstacle of egotism is made easier by the growing insight of those involved in the sharing process that more is achieved with the giving and receiving, with the open exchange, of knowledge, for the networked company but also for the person involved him- or herself than when working in self-imposed and outmoded isolation. In this regard, the patterns of behaviour adopted in research can serve as a model.

A new dimension of creative handling of knowledge is opening up for the human brain, where the tendency to analytical thought and the desire to understand every detail, right down to the finest ramifications of an issue, are fading into the background. The ability of the human being to think is being liberated from mere storage of the traditional knowledge of facts and rules. Knowledge management provides the methodological and technological instruments to handle this process successfully; it is a process which must first be worked through in the heads of the employees, and is only realised as a secondary stage by the provision of a suitable IT system.

It is only the systematic association of information and knowledge from different sources and areas of experience in a creative process which leads to knowledge, in the sense of knowledge management and competence. Information is the raw material of the knowledge economy. The ability to upgrade information to knowledge, so to speak, is becoming a key competence on which success depends. Knowledge workers produce new knowledge by intelligently combining information, insights, models and schemes to produce a higher level of intensification, facilitating new insights. As a result, the company generates available knowledge which can be used and developed, which constitutes an asset – an asset representing a powerful lever for competitive advantage and future growth.

Companies Open up Knowledge as a Strategic Resource

The production and exploitation of knowledge are completed in a feed-back loop with four phases – generation, capture, retrieval and utilisation. The generation phase includes the recording of existing knowledge and the areas where expansion is needed, together with the systematic linking of information to form knowledge. In the capture phase, the knowledge is documented in its functional-logical and contextual associations and knowledge architectures are built up. In the third phase, knowledge is prepared for retrieval, for example through the three-dimensional representation of knowledge landscapes, through free navigation systems and also through zoom functions. Lastly, in phase four the focus moves to targeted support for the use and application of knowledge, while at the same time ensuring permanent maintenance and further development of the knowledge thesaurus. It is immediately noticeable that these are challenging activities for qualified knowledge workers, for people who have the uncommon gift of developed creativity.

Knowledge management can be understood as an answer to the complexity of internal and external factors which have developed rapidly, affecting economic enterprises with increasing speed, bringing about direct change or initiating a need for change.

In knowledge-based industries, a growing number of companies have defined knowledge as a strategic resource, recognised the risk of a loss of knowledge as a result of the new, freer relationship between employees and companies, and are therefore implementing knowledge management processes and forming competence domains. They use their 'organised' knowledge as a lasting competitive advantage. Knowledge-intensive business processes such as marketing programmes (and within this, price marketing and promotional marketing in particular), management of customer relations or strategic purchasing profit especially from well-organised knowledge management. That applies in equal measure to the knowledge-driven area of research, development and innovation. In the modern service society, productivity largely results from the production factor of knowledge. In the past, even major companies were often not aware, or not fully aware, of the value of their intellectual capital in the past. As a result, they could not use it consistently and systematically.

Knowledge management must be understood as an institutionalised and iterative process, through which knowledge is created in a systematic manner, shared and communicated, distributed, used/applied and thus constantly improved and further developed. Knowledge management orients itself using the organic principle of cell division, as it were. The division of knowledge results in new and more broadly based knowledge.

- Knowledge must be made accessible to all employees who need it, instead of leaving it in files or in the head of one individual as in the past.

- Knowledge must be defined clearly and in sufficient detail, so that it is valuable (including for other people).

- Companies must focus their attention on knowledge which is vital for their business.

- Knowledge relevant to the company can only develop its benefits if it is utilised just as systematically as it is gathered together. This means that efficient knowledge management must ensure that knowledge is used.

- Knowledge management is aimed at promoting productivity, creativity and the power to innovate.

Implementing a functioning knowledge management system is only to a small degree an organisational challenge, given the use of modern IT technologies. The decidedly more difficult task is overcoming the human problems, and above all problems of mind-set. Lastly, what is at issue is the introduction of a continuous learning process, which requires even greater efforts to keep it in motion and to develop it further. Knowledge management is work in progress, and never concluded. As with all change processes in companies, when implementing knowledge management systems, a fundamental precondition for success must again be satisfied: top management must have understood that this is a key lever for lasting improvement of company performance, and it must make this commitment convincingly evident to everyone in the company.

Reassessing the Individual as the Carrier of Knowledge

I cannot emphasise too strongly that the extent to which companies are successful in the knowledge society depends critically on whether and to what extent the people factor determines the thinking and actions of top management. Particularly with the introduction of a knowledge management process, one is dealing with a sensitive intervention into human patterns of behaviour which have been passed down over generations. The new, more profound insight into the role of knowledge as the fourth factor in production stands in a logical correlation with the reassessment of the people resource in the company, and with recognition of the status of the individual as a carrier of knowledge, a 'creative centre' and a decision-maker, who introduces his or her own will into the equation.

Three key questions need to be carefully considered and answered before implementation is begun:

- How does one achieve the necessary change of attitude on the part of the employees in the company, so that in future relevant knowledge is generously shared with others?

- Which accompanying organisational development measures are necessary for the launch?

- Which are the most important different initiatives for knowledge management?

The findings from discussions with 65 companies around the world where knowledge management organisations were implemented form the basis for the considerations. A first, general answer to the key questions is that the continuous production of new knowledge demands organisational/personal networking and communications, particularly in the four areas of organisational culture, organisational structure, systems/information technology and measurement systems for knowledge.

As essential elements of organisational culture, the following should be mentioned:

- Alignment to performance management with qualitative objectives at the operational level;

■ Values-based management with defined objectives; and (particularly important in this context)

■ Rewarding that 'unnatural' action which is the making available of personal knowledge, without which the required interaction between employees cannot be achieved.

The organisational structure should ideally display progressive characteristics such as customer-centred business processes, links between the business processes and the utilisation of the lever effects of the extended enterprise.

A precondition for the development of suitable systems and the optimal arrangement of information technology is the identification of the necessary knowledge. This is followed by:

■ Development of an infrastructure for interaction (generally an Intranet);

■ Alignment of the systems to processes, in other words providing the necessary flexibility; and

■ Introduction of an electronic business networking model.

A qualified IT infrastructure is doubtless an indispensable precondition for knowledge management capable of performing the necessary functions, with global access and rapid response times. On the other hand, direct exchanges between knowledge-carriers in personal discussions remain vital.

Measurement systems for knowledge presuppose the development of measures to assess the profitability of knowledge. These should facilitate the measurement of the knowledge content of products and services. Ultimately, it is with the definition of measurement systems that the execution of these 'unnatural acts of generosity' can be observed.

When creating a knowledge programme, it is without doubt of benefit if best practice can be drawn upon. Starting from clearly communicated values and purposes of the organisation, knowledge management should first be introduced into a competence area with particular value and high visibility, because it is important to be able to build on successes. Knowledge management will also constantly access information outside

one's own organisation, because there is far more information available outside the company than within it.

From Implicit to Explicit Knowledge

In addition to this, effective knowledge management requires five activities which are aimed at achieving this 'unnatural act of generosity' already alluded to, onto which further light is to be cast here. Dr Leopold K. Fara of the Paderborn Institute for Applied Psychology differentiates in this context between individual, implicit knowledge – that is, which is present but unavailable – and explicit and available knowledge. He states that the challenge lies in converting implicit to explicit knowledge, since only around 10 per cent of our total capital of knowledge is made available; 90 per cent generally remains unused.[8] This also demonstrates the barriers to overcoming one's natural instincts in this area. What is at issue is no longer viewing the knowledge of employees and groups as a personal possession, but of freeing that knowledge from the individual knowledge carrier and converting it into structural knowledge which is directly accessible for the company. It seems to go against human nature to be prepared to participate in this process:

■ Employees must be encouraged to share their knowledge with others, in other words to make available to others the best of their own thinking and, with that, an important part of their competitive advantage as an individual.

■ They must want to work together, and thus work together on the ideas of other experts.

■ They must be encouraged to share in the work on the process of constant updating and improvement, by helping to draw in new ideas and discoveries continually and by replacing outdated knowledge.

Behind this approach lies the insight from Dr Fara that the assets of a company always include the sum of that which the employees collectively are capable of. Phrased in this way, it demonstrates the potential for added value which is locked in the knowledge stored in employees.

The length of the half-life for knowledge is becoming ever shorter. This is an incentive for employees to engage actively in the process of constant renewal and exchange of knowledge, thereby ensuring that one's own knowledge is always kept up to date. For career-aware young people, a well-developed knowledge management system presents an attractive opportunity of supporting one's own career advancement by participating actively in that system, since the quality of one's participation is noted. In progressive companies, it feeds into the appraisal. Professor Warnecke, President of the Fraunhofer Gesellschaft, is convinced:

> Communication and the ability to learn are becoming key qualities of employees in businesses. In parallel with the traditional training system, a wide variety of multimedia and virtual training offers will be established. Lifelong continuing training will mainly be carried out using multimedia and on a decentralised basis, at home or in the office.[11]

The quality and value of a knowledge-carrier are no longer measured by how much his or her personal knowledge is in advance of others, but – in addition to his or her individual creativity – by the intensity and the readiness to make this knowledge accessible to others. Of course, this particularly applies to the area of research and development, where it is fair to say that there is a tradition of such behaviour.

Knowledge-sharing Needs Incentives

Effective sharing/communication of knowledge cannot be achieved without appropriate training for employees. The training must make clear that everyone who shares knowledge also becomes a participant in the knowledge held by other knowledge-carriers in the company, thereby also enriching him- or herself. Procedures and technologies must support the creation of knowledge. In addition, it is important to measure the influence of knowledge management on the development of business. Lastly, knowledge management must not be allowed to degenerate into a system which is simply self-serving.

Knowledge sharing can be encouraged using a system of incentives for employees. This system should follow a few basic principles:

- Existing incentive systems should be integrated into knowledge management.

- The necessary cultural change in the handling of knowledge should be promoted through visible recognition, acknowledgement and encouragement. Top management must not only be involved, but must also establish clear responsibility for handling knowledge. A knowledge manager should be nominated; teams should be set up on important issues. The advantages and the benefits of knowledge management must be communicated intensively and repeatedly.

- To overcome inhibitions passed down over time, targeted incentives are required to facilitate the provision and active use of knowledge. The options range from staff appraisal and defined career advantages through bonus systems and financial incentives, awards and competitions through to the printing of articles in internal company publications and the authorship of books and articles for an external readership. Participation in special events can also act as an incentive, but at all costs the incentive should be an individual and visible commendation.

Naturally, successful implementation of a permanent knowledge management process is not only dependent on the conduct of employees. Above all, it represents a challenge for the company itself. It must invest in people and systems in order to facilitate the sharing of knowledge and collaboration. James O'Toole, Vice-President of the Aspen Institute and author of several American management books, defined the corporate goal in this area thus:

> Knowledge-based companies will need an entrepreneurial spirit and a culture in which the existing respective levels of performance and knowledge are never considered to be sufficient.[48]

This state of quasi-institutionalised dissatisfaction with one's own performance acts as a tremendous spur to improvement.

The results of the study of 65 companies around the world, referred to earlier in this section, where knowledge management processes have been installed can be summarised in three observations linked to actual practice. These are set out below, because they make it easier for the CEO to implement knowledge management.

Best Practice Summarised

Observation 1 shows that successful companies address the issue of knowledge which offers them competitive advantage and simultaneously makes it possible for them to realise significant strategic improvements in performance and profits. Implementation of the knowledge management process takes place in three stages.

The first stage, entitled *Pro Knowledge*, indicates a position within the company where knowledge is used with little attempt at a systematic approach; rather, it is simply collected and communicated ad hoc.

In the second stage, termed *Return on Investment*, the company improves its knowledge management in one or two areas of core competence, and aspires to make an attractive return on its investment in knowledge. In this stage, competitive advantages arise from the availability of outstanding knowledge – outstanding by comparison with other companies who remain at stage 1.

In the third stage, the company achieves the level of being a *Learning Organisation*. The company aligns itself to rapid improvement of its full spectrum of service, by using knowledge to continually improve some decisions but also to make discontinuous leaps in other decision-making situations. At this stage, competitive advantage depends above all on being able to reach levels of improvements more quickly than the competition.

Observation 2 emphasises and strengthens the conviction I have already expressed, that a change in thinking and attitude is a vital precondition for the success of a knowledge management programme. The people affected account for 90 per cent of the challenge, report the managers tasked with introducing knowledge management programmes. Knowledge is not tangible, and knowledge management is often (still) not well enough understood.

It is *not* about putting knowledge into the 'box' which the mind of another employee represents, but about specifically making knowledge available to those people who need it. Knowledge should not be communicated in a manner which relies on intuition, but defined in a way that is clear and detailed enough to be of value.

Knowledge management aims to drive forward the best shared thinking within the company. This simultaneously results in a focusing on knowledge which is vital for the conduct of business. A very important part in the success of the programme is ensuring that knowledge is also used and not just kept in readiness. If not, the intended permanent process can all too easily stall.

Observation 3 relates to the connection between knowledge management and profits earned by the company, to which ultimately everything else is subordinate. Knowledge management – and its development into a competence network – is not an isolated activity, but the systematic production, use and improvement of strategic information and discoveries which enable the company to operate more efficiently and more effectively. Knowledge proves to be the critical component in *all* business activities, and its influence can be felt right across a broad range of areas including product development, marketing and price-setting. Those who practice knowledge management are generally in agreement that assessment and measurement of the return, that is, that which is earned in return for the investment in knowledge, are increasingly necessary. A typical statement on this point runs:

> Many of us are arguing for business cases to be put together which can be used to quantify the benefits of knowledge management for a company.[51]

Furthermore, the details of this third observation confirm the importance of incentives. In the final analysis, efficient participation in knowledge, without information overload, is what is required. Knowledge must be integrated into daily work. In the main, knowledge management programmes are not successful when effort goes into building up the necessary IT infrastructure, but too little attention is paid to securing the necessary cultural change in behaviour.

There are many reasons identified as causes of failure:

- Important initiatives were launched but change never took place.

- The initiatives were ultimately not that important – regardless of whether change took place or not.

- Knowledge was created, but no 'engine' was developed to support the process of applying this knowledge.

- Information systems were installed, but there was no lasting stimulus to generate knowledge.

The change in employee behaviour will not work – as has already been demonstrated – without incentives for the employees concerned/involved. When looking for the causes as to why a knowledge management programme was not successful, consultants paid critical attention to the issue of the existing incentive systems. They found serious weaknesses, for example there were incentive systems which did not encourage staff to engage in active 'knowledge sharing':

- Because there was no clear financial reward for sharing knowledge;

- Because readiness to share knowledge is not a subject included in the institution's appraisal system;

- Because the exchange of knowledge is not supported by established processes and technologies;

- Because the benefit of knowledge management within the company is neither measured nor communicated.

These few points alone indicate the direction to be taken if one is to avoid developing a programme which is not up to the task.

Proactive Knowledge Management

Most knowledge management initiatives are reactive, because knowledge is often produced as a result of past business, and because there is no attempt to arrive at it progressively and to improve it through collective efforts (for example, by drawing in experts who are not involved in

the relevant activity, and who therefore approach it with a fresh eye). Competence networks (see Chapter 4) facilitate proactive knowledge management. They help to create an environment which encourages continual exchange about what is needed for the future, and close collaboration over satisfying these future requirements. Participants involved in the day-to-day business are involved in the production and use of knowledge. Participants can find support for specific problems. Active suppliers can be recognised more easily and third parties (for example consultants) can be involved without effort.

The status accorded to customer orientation in the spectrum of management challenges has already been discussed. Networks of people are also an outstanding tool for encouraging thinking in terms of customer categories and for practical customer orientation. On the one hand, marketing and sales staff can access concentrated knowledge within the network and immediately become aware of every aspect of product and service improvements. On the other hand, customer information serves as feedback to the organisation, and customers are given controlled access to company knowledge. That increases their level of awareness and their satisfaction. Finally, managers in marketing, sales and also in product management and customer services share in knowledge about customer problems, and can react faster and in a more focused manner. Practical improvement of service quality via the network begins with the establishment of special competence domains for sales and marketing staff, and continues with the possibility of linking in with back office services. Customers have access to selected corporate competence domains. A further option is to create special competence domains via which customers and sales staff can communicate with one another interactively.

This example alone shows clearly that collaboration in networks can effortlessly go beyond internal company boundaries. For many companies, their ability to compete is directly related to their ability to network. First, such networks enable employees with different levels of responsibility to be brought into contact with clients, suppliers and partner companies. Second, they offer almost unlimited opportunities to share selected, controlled knowledge 'across boundaries'.

Knowledge networks and human networks are not limited to companies. Their development and operation can, for example, also include

scientific institutes, research laboratories within companies and educational institutions. There are already many initiatives developing knowledge networks. The aim is to create knowledge markets in the Internet, which network existing islands of knowledge and generate a high utility value for users in the fields of science, the economy and for the general public through new optical and logical structures. Here we are often talking about strategic offensives, such as in the approach of the Bavarian government, for example, which is looking to develop Bavaria as a high-tech location suited to the demands of the knowledge society in the 21st century. The experts at the Fraunhofer Gesellschaft are also convinced that the co-operations and strategic alliances in research and development must become more deeply embedded in order to link institutionally and regionally distributed competence centres efficiently. Whether the network is internal to the company or a public regional network, for the employees involved the shared and responsible development of knowledge represents in either case an interesting expansion to and enrichment of their own individual sphere of action. They are drawn into the creative centre of a learning organisation, and they regenerate and update their own knowledge at the same time. They need have no fears regarding their 'employability'.

CHAPTER 4

Lasting Success

Lasting success can only be achieved if companies work to create the preconditions and the basis for establishing that success. Addressing the symptoms alone can at best achieve short-term cures, but cannot bring about long-term change.

As should be apparent from the preceding chapters, individuals as carriers of knowledge and creativity, combined with people-focused management, constitute the key precondition for corporate success in the 21st century. Only where these preconditions are met can companies successfully come through new challenges and adapt flexibly to changing framework conditions. Why should companies continue to be structured along the lines developed by Frederick Winslow Taylor 100 years ago?[45]

A simple 'Think – Talk – Do' matrix can ensure that important principles are respected with regard to the central importance of the people factor in those change processes to which companies are permanently subjected. I had the opportunity to develop this matrix at an international workshop with Booz Allen Hamilton partners from around the world and with James O'Toole,[40] the former Vice-President of the Aspen Institute. Participation in the workshop started from the central question: 'How are change processes successfully set in motion, led and implemented?'

For these five aspects – key principles, understanding the problem, vision/objectives, the role of employees, and the change process – participants elaborated criteria and guidance for actions, within a framework of consistency in actions, which lead to an expectation of the

greatest success in the implementation of change processes. The statements made by the workshop participants about the 'most important principles', summarised in the table below, demonstrate how accurately Professor Dr Rupert Lay has described the key demand made of top managers, 'that he is an honest person'. In all change processes, a critical success factor is honesty, which generates credibility.

Immediately after the personal qualities of the top manager – honesty, fairness, openness – participants identified the ability to weigh up carefully the interests of shareholders, employees and management, and suppliers and customers as part of stakeholder value, and to reassess that balance regularly. It has already been demonstrated that in achieving this balance, the manager is critically dependent on the readi-

Leadership Framework – Leadership for Change			
	'Think'	'Talk'	'Do'

1. Key principles	■ Openness/honesty
	■ Fairness
	■ Stakeholder objective (for example profitability)
		■ At every opportunity
		  – in public
		  – in small groups
		  – one-on-one
		■ Two way
		■ Go to them (do not make them come to you)
			■ Act consistently with principles
			
			■ Recognise and reward appropriate behaviour
			
			■ Punish inappropriate behaviour
			
			■ Initiate key processes
			
			■ Lead by example
			
			■ Encourage input outside the hierarchy
			
			■ Be flexible with tactics, inflexible on principles

2. Understanding the problem	■ Objectivity ■ Data-based ■ Root causes/ constraints	■ Build awareness of and consensus around problem ■ Focus on opportunity not fault	
3. Vision/objectives	■ How is it different? ■ Why will we win? ■ What is in it for us all?	■ Simple ■ Focused ■ Consistent ■ Shared ■ Personal	
4. Role of employees	■ Understand real motivation and needs ■ Discover how to communicate effectively	■ Achieving the overall goal will benefit the whole group ■ Set expectations ■ Create followers/ champions	
5. Change process	■ Delegate wherever possible ... trust your team ■ Play to people's strengths	■ Minimal	■ Delegate, empower ... and get out of the way

Source: Booz Allen Hamilton

ness of all interest groups to moderate their demands in accordance with the situation. Shareholder value, properly understood, can only be realised on a lasting basis if stakeholders find that their interests are taken into consideration.

Of course, this balance of interests presupposes full and profound understanding of the problems and a desire to achieve objectivity. It goes without saying that analytical investigations and insights must be based on sound data. Added to this is the need to get to the root of the problem, not being satisfied with merely finding superficial symptoms and 'fixing' these with cosmetic measures, but instead addressing the fundamental roots of the situation. Only in this way can the objective and direction of the necessary change be soundly based and defined.

Once this is in place, the further steps in the analytical thought process are set out, as outlined in the table. The questions about the specific position of the company ('How is it different?') and about the strategy which promises success ('Why will we win?') are extended in the next stage to take on board the perspective of stakeholder value: 'What is in it for us all?'

For large organisations, long-term objectives, including change objectives, can only be reached if top managers succeed in winning followers, to use the sector jargon. A precondition for developing employees as change agents is that they understand, take on board and accept the need for the change. If they can see in change an opportunity for themselves, a professional opportunity, and agreement with their own objectives, then it is not difficult to motivate them.

To that end, more than ever before the manager must develop and make use of the ability to communicate. Ultimately, the motivational words must be accompanied by credible actions. The key words in the table speak for themselves: delegate, encourage confidence, empower employees.

The status accorded to communication, to 'talking things through', was very clearly expressed in a session facilitated by O'Toole, which saw a separate column dedicated to the issue of 'Talk' being included in the table. The content of that column requires no commentary, and neither do the recommendations for action in the 'Do' column.

When it comes to implementation of major changes, the main element lacking in companies is still often the dynamic processes or

deliberately introduced means of circumventing the hierarchy, for example in the form of project teams which the CEO establishes for a period somewhere within the company and which report directly to him or her. Even today, in the traditional-style German company, there are still three tiers of management across the various levels, which more often than not make the work of the project teams on important issues more difficult rather than easier. The often interesting conclusions of the work of these teams can frequently be held up somewhere along the line of command, even in those companies where the management board is attempting to live out its progressive principles. Findings are blocked by those who were not involved in the project work, or who fear for their positions or their responsibilities. The larger the company, the greater the danger of these initiatives fizzling out. The best results are achieved where the CEO or top management appoints teams which cut across all hierarchies and report directly to him or her. In such teams, even young people can participate, people who perhaps have only been with the company for one or two years. In Germany, this form of destructuring is still used far too rarely, in my opinion. The creation and shaping of applications-oriented teams is a good example of the competence and skill needed to bring together different specialists with their specific knowledge and ways of doing things. In this process, flexibility is the key ingredient.

In his book *The Corrosion of Character: The Personal Consequences of Work in the New Capitalism* (published in German under the more neutral title of *The Flexible Individual – The Culture of the New Capitalism*),[35] the American sociologist Richard Sennett demonstrated, to borrow a phrase from Horx, how one 'transforms a magical word of the modern age into a non-word'. Sennett believes that:

> The modern usage of the word 'flexibility' masks a power system ... It should be the essence of flexible change to free oneself from the past and to change what has gone before decisively and irrevocably. With the attack on routine, a new freedom of time is appearing, but its appearance is deceptive. Time in the company and for the individual has been released from the iron cage of the past, but subjected to new controls and new monitoring from above. The era of flexibility is the era of a new power.

Sennett illustrates what he means by that using the example of flexible working time. From this phenomenon, which is nothing other than the person-centred reaction of companies to the needs of self-aware and self-determining employees with their new understanding of individuality and family, of freedom and career, Sennett derives a different and more sinister meaning: 'If flexible working time is a privilege bestowed by the employer, then it is also a new form of his power.'

Sennett postulates that the most flexible form of working time, home working, is causing great disquiet among employers. In Germany, this disquiet has – up until now, at any rate – always found hostile expression from the trade union side, and not from the company side. It is certainly true that fragmentation and flexibility are accompanied by problems which affect people directly, even if they do not lead to the 'corrosion of character'[35] and loss of individuality, as the American sociologist exaggeratedly fears. However, the person-centred aspect of modern corporate management must be directed towards countering such dangers in a proactive manner. Making this clear is the central concern of this book.

Keeping a Human Scale with Ambitious Objectives

Destructuring and at the same time achieving greater flexibility also means changing the corporate culture, and demanding new patterns of behaviour from employees. The challenge is to form an integrated structure out of the many associated parts of the company which is moving in the same direction. This cannot be achieved without the commitment of the CEO and the globally aligned top management. And this complex task is naturally best handled by the type of top manager who has a breadth of knowledge gained from experience, who has wide life knowledge and a broad cultural horizon. Even the tough and charismatic CEO Jack Welch, who over the past two decades has shaken up GE from the bottom up and spurred the company on to new and higher levels of performance, recently acknowledged: 'You have to work on the edge of madness.'[21] That means that at the same time there is a potential risk of values becoming lost. Top managers looking for lasting success must be very clearly aware of this connection. Ambitious objec-

tives come up against their limits where they fail to respect the people factor. Ethical values and respect for the worth of the individual play a decisive role in this.

It goes without saying that a culture or the value of customer orientation, for example, can be realised more easily in networked companies with many small units which each have their own identity. The greater the number of such units, as for example at Philips or ABB, where the national organisations were or are also largely structured into divisions or independent legal entities, the more important it is to take parallel moves to establish and promote the commonalities – the binding, overarching elements – and define and maintain the values of the company. If not, there is a real danger that what becomes established is simply a series of small kingdoms and petty fiefdoms, which have a surprising life of their own, with a developed sense of self-importance and flamboyance, even going as far as developing an independent company logo. If this is the case, then the synergistic advantages of the major corporation, such as higher efficiency, brand positioning and a common market presence can easily slip – with potentially dire consequences for the overall image perceived by customers and partners in the extended enterprise. Currently a return to powerful common values, objectives and functions can be observed taking place in many companies which have undergone a phase of extreme divisionalisation.

Between Differentiation and Standardisation

More and more often, therefore, large corporations adopt a third form of organisational unit in order to exploit synergy effects, namely shared services. This unit brings together all those activities which do not constitute differentiating characteristics for the market, and which are not required to react to differences between customer groups. Typical of this type of activity is joint procurement, for example of office materials, or the processing of all kinds of financial transactions. One can certainly see a parallel here with the platform strategy in the automobile construction sector. In both instances, the approach aims at cost-efficient standardisation, as far as is possible, of everything which remains invisible for the customer/user and does not contribute to differentiating the

product in the market. Of course, it is all the more important to emphasise those differentiating features of the product and the market-oriented units which are aimed at the customer. The ease with which it is possible to overstep the boundaries in this area can be demonstrated by, for example, the criticism levelled by motoring journalists at certain details of the interior of the new Jaguar S 400, on account of the use of equivalent parts from the standard Ford construction kit which lacked sufficient 'quality'. Even for shared services it is very important to pay careful respect to cultural, linguistic and legislative differences.

The inherent conflict between common values and objectives on the one hand and far-reaching delegation of responsibility to the market-oriented units on the other – in accordance with the developing insight of companies – can only be resolved if common objectives and a common cultural understanding of values are used to ensure that all those involved are moving in a single direction, with the customer-oriented units at the same time aligning themselves clearly and consistently with their local customers, their country-specific needs, their differentiating aspects and their cultural specificities. For that reason, it is in fact counterproductive, not to say nonsensical, to preach 'values' on the one hand but to act as a centralist organisation on the other. In a clear division of tasks, and without moving to exercise control wholly at the local/regional level, the head office should be responsible above all for tasks which have a general application, such as developing and permanently adapting the overall strategy, defining the objectives and the framework for investment and the global public presence; it should concern itself with the corporate culture, values and identity and other central issues such as public relations.

Developing and maintaining openness towards individuals and their creative ideas rank among the major opportunities and challenges of a new, open corporate culture which is shaped by this approach. In practical terms, this means that in the company, everyone must know that he or she can put forward ideas without restrictions and without having to worry about doing so, even where, at first sight, these ideas might appear to be somewhat comical but may contain an element which is of interest and might perhaps prove a fruitful stimulus for the company. And the employee must know that no personal disadvantage will derive from this, that – on the contrary – managers and colleagues are appreciative of

the fact that someone thinks independently. It also requires that the reporting structure in the company is permeable and open. Many ideas are blocked, suppressed or – for whatever reason – incorrectly assessed on the route through the various levels of the hierarchy, especially at middle management level, which is often referred to as the 'clay layer'. It is not unusual for middle management to incorrectly regard one of its tasks as being to select, filter and therefore also manipulate the information flow between 'the ground level', where business life is pulsating and the market makes its demands, and 'the top level', where the management teams take decisions. This often extreme filter function depends strongly on political status within the company, especially if passing on interesting ideas and information is understood to be an action which jeopardises one's own position. However nonsensical such fears and worries might be, they can have a negative effect. The second key influencing factor is the individual personality of the middle manager. The more developed, the more independent his or her thinking and actions, the easier it will be for that middle manager to exercise the filter function liberally, keep the filter more permeable, and avoid blockages. To spell it out – he or she will search for and find the best ideas without feeling threatened by doing so. Again, it is evident that the highest management challenge of today and tomorrow is to change human behaviour and break up those ossified structures within which whole generations have comfortably been able to accommodate themselves. Managers lacking in the people factor will fail in this task in the long term.

An outdated but widely held attitude, particularly among insecure managers who fear for their position, when considering any process or any new idea, is to ask first of all whether it will benefit, or can at least do no harm to, the manager him- or herself. This ingrained attitude, which is geared to producing a preventative mind-set, must be changed into a realisation that everything which benefits the company will ultimately also benefit the manager. Recently, this constructive thinking has also been emerging in Germany, for example finding expression in stock options programmes which knowledge-based companies such as SAP are using, with a view to committing their management and knowledge-carriers more strongly to the company. In the USA, such programmes have for a number of years been a proven method of promoting entrepreneurial thinking within the company and rewarding employee

loyalty. If the belief that there is a harmony of interests between management and the company has already permeated through, then it is a lot easier for everyone to work alongside one another since the people are operating and meeting one another with a higher level of freedom within the company.

Central protection and control structures, which have been built up in German companies and elsewhere, almost always get in the way of the power to innovate. Typical of conservative product development processes is the small number of new abilities or competences and the large number of products which are developed purely as derivatives of existing concepts. While it is true that under these traditional processes projects which cannot demonstrate their economic potential are eliminated at an early stage, there is too little room allowed for creativity and visions to flourish. In the short term, the traditional 'funnel process' may lead to very good results, but in the medium and long term it fails to deliver those truly new products with high potential which ultimately secure growth.

An Approach which Promises Success: The Market Development Manager

One approach which is being used with lasting success is, as has already been briefly outlined, the introduction of a post with responsibility for the market launch of new products, namely that of the creative 'market development manager'. This new type of manager is generally drawn not from the technological management side, but from the product management area. He or she assumes responsibility for a market area and can select interesting concepts for this market area (exercising a budget-holding responsibility in this regard), and take these concepts through the initial stages of product development or new business development. He or she is empowered, not least by being allocated available funding, to support the projects which in his or her judgement satisfy the demands of the market. He or she initiates the championing of concepts through a business funding process.

A vital precondition for rapid and cost-effective product development is effective focus on the market. With the aid of this focus, products

which will have only limited success can be avoided; no expenditure is wasted on things which are only marginally important for customers. Establishing creativity within the company is not enough on its own. There must also be a guarantee of responsibility and support for new ideas. The new post of the market development manager with his or her own 'seed' budget establishes this responsibility at a very early stage. Admittedly, the closer the idea comes to launch on the market, and depending on the particular scale, a series of processes and structures are needed which release both the financial and the human resources for this idea. This is the aim of the review and sponsoring process which I cannot address in further detail here, but which has been described extensively by Marc Powell and Barry Jaruzelski.[41]

Among the special challenges for top management is the radical paradigm shift which precedes the transformation from a technology-driven to a market-driven company, together with the practical implementation of that change in manageable stages. Traditional German company groups have been technology-driven for generations. These groups often began with ground-breaking inventions by typical inventor-entrepreneurs: the car, invented by Carl Benz and Gottlieb Daimler, the seamless pipe by the Mannesmann brothers, magneto ignition by Robert Bosch, telegraphy by Werner von Siemens, and standard software for company management by SAP. The shift to becoming a market-driven company has caused many of these companies considerable problems – and some are still experiencing problems today. By contrast, this shift was easier for entrepreneur-founded companies which were, from the outset, geared to the marketing of products manufactured under licence, and which were therefore more strongly aligned with the market and its constantly changing demands.

When companies realise that their own technological and staffing resources are not sufficient to realise the rapid flow of marketable innovations, required above all in modern high-tech growth sectors, innovation sourcing can prove an appropriate route for acquiring the necessary competences and capacities. The American network specialist Cisco, for a long time one of the stars of the American stock market firmament, offers an impressive example of the success of this strategy. The *New York Times* has characterised the method of thinking and working at Cisco succinctly and accurately: 'Cisco has a simple strategy: if their

own in-house engineers cannot create a technology – of whatever kind – then they buy it.' Cisco uses acquisitions to secure knowledge and talent which serve the whole company. This can be clearly demonstrated from the fact that this company has acquired more than 20 SMEs within a 30-month period. Today it can be confirmed that the integration of almost all these companies has been successful – not least because Cisco places value on preserving the culture of a start-up. Another reason is that the former owners of the companies acquired are given management positions by Cisco and are signed up at an early stage to common objectives and values. Since the massive fall in prices of stocks and therefore the loss of this 'acquisition currency' this run of success was suspended.

One of the results of this strategy is that today around 40 per cent of expenditure for research and development at Cisco is 'outsourced'. A logical consequence of this is that in-house development has been reduced. For large companies, which are rich in tradition and technologically oriented but where the power to innovate is showing signs of certain deficiencies, innovation sourcing can be an effective strategy to achieve improvements in innovation flow and marketing of innovations in the relatively short term. In such instances it is worth reflecting on the new alignment required of the research and development process to take account of the increasing external procurement of innovative products, solutions, teams with major expertise or whole companies. By implementing best practice from successful competitors, through the integration of the culture and processes of acquired start-ups, it is possible to achieve notable progress. There is, however, a need to develop a strategy for active management of the innovation portfolio. Finally, the provision of risk capital and management expertise for start-ups belongs to the repertoire of possible measures. Siemens AG provides an interesting example with its Siemens Venture Capital GmbH, a company formally established a few years ago, through which it is intensifying its activities in this field.

Dirk R. Lupenberger describes the basic idea of his business using a metaphor: 'small venture companies must learn to dance with the elephant – and vice versa.'[42] As a summary of its activities, Siemens Venture Capital has invested more than €100 million directly or indirectly via funds in promising start-ups. Siemens employees who go independent to pursue their own inventions and business ideas have

also been among the group of start-ups supported. Other major companies such as Deutsche Telekom AG are also active in the venture capital market.

Powerful Impetus for Young Start-ups

Company start-ups, for example those receiving venture capital support from Siemens or Telekom, have proved for a couple of years to be one of the most powerful engines worldwide, not only for market-oriented innovations but also for the creation of new jobs. Conversely, the lack of adequate support for start-ups in the past, given a climate marked by an extremely cautious mind-set on the part of the money-providers, is one of the reasons why in Germany there were too few new jobs created with young, innovative companies, until the start of the 'New Market' segment of the stock market. Since then there has been a fundamentally positive change in the situation – if one excludes the over-hyped ventures which exacted a bitter revenge on gullible or easily persuaded investors. Comparative international studies, such as those carried out by Booz Allen Hamilton, show that the availability of venture capital (often called risk capital in Germany, which tends to cast it in a negative light) is one of the decisive factors for the foundation of new companies with a high potential to innovate, and is often the factor which makes it possible at all. The creation of new jobs in the USA correlates directly with the more straightforward and ready availability of venture capital there. Of course, another important question relates to the areas in which venture capital is invested. In the USA, two-thirds of such funding is directed towards high technology areas, whereas in Germany prior to the innovative start of the New Market it was less than a fifth – and that in a context of a significantly lower volume of investment overall. In other words, there is a need for a greater readiness to take risk. Nevertheless, the trend over recent years entitles the observer to have cautious optimism in this regard.

In the era of the Internet society of the new millennium, growth is achieved under new and tougher conditions – first with greater speed and dynamism, and second under an ever-present threat as a result of almost complete transparency in global competition, with ever-more

rapid reactions to temporary competitive advantages. The staggering pace of development in e-Business provides a living lesson for these contexts. Yet, at the same time, e-Business is a good example of the opportunities for growth afforded by the Internet, which arise from new business ideas. Companies engaging in a systematic search for new business ideas and the targeted development of these ideas to render them fit for market – ideally under the guiding hand of market development managers – profit disproportionately from this activity. In particular, this will be the case if they succeed in transferring existing core competences, among which their competence in respect of the market ranks highly, to new business areas.

Organic growth under one's own efforts – most likely to be achieved with the aid of a constant stream of innovations which are fit for market – is without doubt a sound way, but at the same time it is just one way among several to achieve the desired company size. Some young businesses, particularly start-ups in the high tech and software industry, have gone about this task at breathtaking speed within the boom years of the New Economy, with annual growth rates above 50 per cent. But even in these growth sectors, whose development was reflected in the indices of the NASDAQ and the New Market, acquisitions were on the agenda – so long as investors played along and financed the expansion. Their readiness to invest was ultimately determined by the pragmatic prospect of realising profits, and not by some imaginative business plans as quite a few of the young companies have to painfully experience. Investors and providers of venture capital have become far more cautious in recent times, in the face of the increasing numbers of collapses of Internet companies. Postponed IPOs are an unmistakable sign of this new and sober attitude. But this must not be allowed to lead to a return to risk-averse methods of procedure which seek security above all else.

Acceptance of Mistakes Means Creating Space for Creativity

From managers whose profile fits the selection criteria for a top manager with high demands of him- or herself and of employees, a highly developed sense of how to handle corporate readiness to

embrace risk is expected today and in the future; that personal quality will be marked equally by an awareness and tolerance of risk. The readiness to embrace risk also includes the need to let mistakes happen, because only in this way can the space for creativity be developed. Anyone who wants to be successful must accept mistakes, because one learns from them. A world free of mistakes is a static and unprogressive world, in which companies have no future.

In other words, entrepreneurs who are not prepared to take risks have little opportunity of setting anything into motion. Aversion to risk is almost always based on weakness over decision-making. At the same time, it is one of the serious causes of slowness which can threaten the existence of a company. Readiness to take risk does not exclude an awareness of risk. Where this awareness has been lacking, there have been significant difficulties in recent years – particularly in the banking sector, but also in the construction industry – even leading to the loss of independence for formerly renowned institutes and businesses, to say nothing of the loss of corresponding positions on supervisory and management boards. In both sectors, it is noticeable that the damage occurred particularly in the property sector, where the revenue prospects of construction projects were often overestimated in a bout of optimistic euphoria. With the construction boom in the 'new Federal States' in Eastern Germany following German reunification, the number of instances of this rose – through to the last major crash, the collapse of Holzmann AG. The total collapse at Holzmann could only be postponed, but not avoided, through massive state intervention. Having had its fingers burned, the finance industry reacted wisely – albeit belatedly – by introducing more stringent risk management.

However, within many companies in recent years (at least, up until the formation of the 'New Market' segment of the stock market) there was below-average development of even a calculated readiness to take risk – mainly in respect of innovations, and to a lesser extent in respect of valuation issues. That applies above all to the necessary investment in start-ups, particularly in Germany, which until the sometimes too powerful impetus to growth given by the Net economy enjoyed far fewer development opportunities than for example, the USA, given Germany's limited readiness to take risk and the concomitant unavailability of venture capital. Traditional money lenders still have a safety-first mentality when

it comes to start-ups, which allows even the best business ideas to fail. By asking for the family home to be put up as security, the banks will achieve only one thing: that a prospect full of hope is stifled at birth. Naturally, the readiness to take risk also includes a careful assessment of the opportunities for a new business idea. The high number of venture capital companies has to ensure a better balance between support for start-ups and good business sense. They must support promising business ideas and start-ups with capital as well as good advice.

Readiness to Take Risk is Still Underdeveloped in Germany

Manfred Remmel, Chairman of the Board at RWE Energie AG in 1999 and with previous experience of working in the intensively competitive German automotive industry, also agrees that there is not sufficient willingness to take risk in Germany, and he makes the case for greater courage when it comes to risk, which he believes should be viewed as a challenge and an opportunity. Remmel holds that there is a tendency to view risks per se in absolute terms for only their negative connotations: 'Perception of risk in this way leads inevitably to missed opportunities.'[43] The German tendency to shy away from risk altogether extends into the highest levels of management. Here Remmel refers to Niklas Luhmann's exemplary distinction: 'Since the invention of the umbrella there is still a risk, but no longer a danger, of getting wet.'[43] Risks can be guarded against through one's own decisions and actions.

Hans Dietmar Bürgel, Professor for Research and Development Management at Stuttgart University, has defined seven elements for evaluating risk in research and development, an area where without risk one might as well immediately cease all activities. Bürgel is convinced that the prime element is defining the target market and determining the critical risk thresholds (see section 3.6). The decision to stop pursuing a development is normally a far harder one than approving new funds to continue with the project, since it always involves psychological factors and aspects involving the hierarchy. Who likes admitting that their research or development initiative will not lead to the desired result? Moreover, there are sufficient examples to show that breaking off a development project is associated with painful career adjustment.

As a result, there is a great inclination to rely on the hope fact continue with a project even as it is dawning on the researchers and developers involved that they will not make progress by pursuing the current approach. Considerable risks attach to this understandably human pattern of behaviour. But in such instances the people factor is only influencing the responsible development manager on a personal and not a management level, since otherwise such failed developments would be viewed as a learning opportunity for the company and not assessed negatively.

However, it is not only in research and development and innovation processes where it is critical that the abilities and competences of staff are developed. In general terms, competence is the basis for success, and – not least in order to avoid incalculable risks – the often-cited knowledge society needs new competence networks. These networks will only function if they are strengthened through human networking.

Knowledge which Leads to Competence

If knowledge management is operated successfully and continuously, competence networks develop almost of necessity in place of islands of competence, as a result of the active development and maintenance of knowledge as an asset used by a variety of staff.

Competence, one of the key concepts of contemporary management philosophies, can be defined as the result of an intelligent, active combination of knowledge (understood in the broad sense of the word), experience and personal networks. Competence can be made accessible to others, but it cannot be formalised – and the transfer of competence is labour-intensive, given the high degree of complexity involved. A particularly vital aspect of competence is that if knowledge-carriers leave a company, the competence can dissolve into nothingness. Competence domains can prove to be an effective protection to guard against this latent risk. Booz Allen Hamilton take the term 'competence domain' (in mathematics terminology, domain describes the area of a function) to mean a community of competence-carriers which feeds and supports a network of competence-users, who for their part also integrate knowledge from external knowledge providers and other competence

domains into their work. The competence domain creates and maintains knowledge in the sense of providing knowledge management, as has already been referred to, but in addition to this it also provides support for training. The competence-carriers in a domain understand one another and function as a source of creativity, and ultimately can also supplement other competence domains. They often act as a 'collection point' and a 'marshalling yard' for competences which are made available from other competence domains within or outside the business.

Competence domains must make available a clear added value to their members, through a set of shared services. They must form an effective source of information, practically constituting a common treasury of knowledge, so to speak. As real communities, they must offer contacts to others and help for other members in the company – including, for example, serving as stimulating and productive discussion forums. Competence domains must empower the competence-carriers involved with them to develop their own competences, or to expand their areas of competence. The benefits sketched out here can only be achieved with effective management and clear leadership of the competence domains. For progressive companies, successful competence domains are proving to be a powerful source of professional development, and lead to recognition for the individual in his or her job, thus providing a high level of motivation for their members in a stimulating exchange of giving and receiving.

In practice, competence domains are proving to be extraordinarily flexible structures which can be created in a multiplicity of forms. They can be formed to operate right across dominant organisational structures and processes or to support existing structures and processes. Naturally, they can also involve people with different profiles of knowledge and competences, in other words operating on an interdisciplinary basis, forming virtual project teams in the age of the I-World, so to speak. Most knowledge workers will function in competence domains both as competence-carriers and competence-users. And in both capacities, every individual can belong to several competence domains which offer mutual support to one another. The better networked they are, the more effectively they can work.

Competence networks are a fitting response to the essential challenges which modern organisations must confront. They support:

- The productivity of knowledge workers;

- The manoeuvrability, flexibility and adaptability of the organisation;

- The development of employees as individuals;

- Innovation management;

- A more profound understanding of the market – not least through precise knowledge of the competition and its activities;

- The management of core competences;

- The quality of customer service;

- Networking beyond the boundaries of the organisation;

- The preparation of the organisation for e-Business.

Each of these statements can be backed up with more detailed information and more profound considerations. This list alone suffices to show the extent to which knowledge management and competence networks penetrate a company and enable it to achieve greater performance, because as a result that most valuable of all resources, the individual, is judged in accordance with his or her abilities, drawn into the work and supported as an individual at the same time.

Competence Networks Facilitate Mutual Support

It is apparent that competence networks have a positive influence on the productivity of knowledge workers; this productivity impacts on both the revenue side and costs. In an age of increasing specialisation, knowledge workers must handle growing volumes of knowledge. At the same time, the complexity of that knowledge is increasing and there is a veritable explosion in sources of information. Interdisciplinary working is an absolute necessity. On the other hand, the productivity of knowledge workers is held back by a variety of influences. These include labour-intensive routine tasks such as the gathering of frequently recurring information and elements of knowledge when working in a network with equals and other users. It can also be difficult to recognise the expertise

of others clearly. If aids to working and knowledge are not adequately distributed, then this can easily lead to the notorious 'not invented here' attitude or to a 'do it yourself' mentality. Competence networks enable knowledge workers to rely on common support when searching for information and, by the same standard, to communicate their own expertise more effectively. A network also makes it easier to identify the expertise of equals and external participants, and to have a share in a wealth of resources of both knowledge and tools. As a result, one can concentrate more effectively on activities which add value.

Nor does it require any special imagination to see that competence networks also improve the manoeuvrability of organisations. This manoeuvrability and flexibility have become a key factor in corporate survival and in the realisation of competitive advantages. Companies can identify changes in the market and in the competition at a sufficiently early stage. They can shorten the critical time to market considerably, and improve their ability to respond. In order to achieve this degree of agility, companies must develop a sixth sense, so to speak, so that they recognise possible changes in their environment as early as possible. Information about such changes must be communicated around the company very rapidly. Companies should also develop the ability to mobilise rapidly resources within the organisation and beyond its immediate control, and to develop these for itself. Task forces must operate across the internal boundaries and levels of hierarchy within the organisation, and sometimes over extended time-frames.

Competence networks therefore offer a variety of benefits to improve agility. The awareness of changes, which announce themselves only quietly and barely noticeably but which can be critically important, now takes place at the level of highest competence (which is not necessarily synonymous with the highest level of responsibility in the management). Internal communication operates more rapidly and with a stronger focus. Employees with well-developed outside contacts, and also outside consultants, clients and suppliers can be involved more effectively in developing a company's own strategy. There is precise knowledge of where the reserves of competence are located, and it is possible to install new task forces in the form of competence domains very rapidly.

As early as 1986, long before anyone could have conceived of the possibility of the Internet changing from being a university network for

an élite to become a world-encompassing medium for millions of individuals, Gertrud Höhler described the effects of information technologies on the globalisation of human thinking:

> The information systems gradually carry us around the globe, so that our straightforward connection to the place where we live becomes mixed with the spatial multi-layering of the places where we reside in our minds. Daily challenged to transport ourselves to many places around the world, we also develop a lasting consciousness of mastery over spatial confines.[10]

Höhler was not thinking especially of managers in making this statement, but of people sitting in front of their television screens. How much more valid is her sentence, however, when applied to the development of a lasting global consciousness in the heads of top managers in globally operating companies, whose daily professional life involves 'transporting themselves to many places around the world' every day.

Competence networks support not only the respective company, but equally, and in a complex manner, the development of employees and thus ultimately the competitive ability of the whole company. Staff development has acquired the status of an important competitive advantage, now that it has been understood that employees are the most valuable asset within organisations. At the same time, employees are increasingly prepared for and expect to take responsibility themselves for their own career development. Professional recognition must include both soft skills and hard expertise in equal measure. However, the challenges are becoming greater. Increasing specialisation makes it more difficult to provide a tailored approach to employees, and the individual expectations of the respective job differ more and more. Employee mobility makes it more difficult for companies to keep their competences stable.

Developing One's Own Expertise

On the other hand, staff development can also be supported in a variety of ways by competence networks. Thus, for example, employees can make contact with specific competence domains, in order to develop their own expertise in areas of interest to them on an ongoing basis.

They can also develop their own knowledge of key competence profiles, in other words they can acquire knowledge which is characteristic of particular areas. In addition to this, they can also involve themselves in centres for best practice, knowledge and leadership. It is immediately apparent that competence networks promote the interaction between 'gurus' and learners, and that they keep the latest information available about the existing competition. The network offers the company the opportunity to recognise the special contributions of employees in key areas and to acknowledge this accordingly. The effect of departments on employees can be assessed, so that internal implementation projects or the appointment of new employees can be planned more reliably.

If one is aware of the close correlation between knowledge, creativity and the power to innovate, then it automatically follows that competence networks support and make easier the task of innovation management. Effective management of innovations facilitates initiatives by individuals or teams – naturally, within the context of a common direction. It supports different disciplines in working together, and encourages extended but effective access to information from outside. Innovation management facilitates management via a portfolio structure which involves different time horizons and core competences. In addition, it is characteristic of modern innovation management that it encourages people to pursue careers as experts and not just in management – and this too is again a very positive aspect in terms of the people factor.

Common Basis of Current Knowledge

Competence networks contribute to the effective management of innovations by providing meeting places and opportunities for communication for new initiatives, building bridges between different competence domains and making available highly qualified sources of information for common use. Within the competence network, a shared database of knowledge is organised, enriched and maintained. Top management has the opportunity to introduce new competence domains and align them to important strategic objectives, and to open up new career opportunities.

Competence centres can provide outstanding services for the systematic procurement, selection, gathering and evaluation of data and infor-

mation about the competitive environment of the company (called 'business intelligence' for short), whether in terms of keeping permanent tabs on the competition, monitoring market trends or keeping a watchful eye at all times on technological development. The obstacles to such continuous monitoring are the variety of boundaries which one comes up against, and the wealth of information, much of which is redundant and with gaps in the quality. Also there are often problems with the internal communication of information illustrating changes. In many instances, the information is not sufficiently adapted to the needs of the company and therefore does not provide sufficiently intensive support for change management. Competence networks can be an effective aid in this area. Routine activities are concentrated as a central service in a competence domain. Feedback and discussion rounds on individual processes are supported by simple mechanisms, and external suppliers of information are actively integrated into the process.

Core competences – to which repeated reference is made in this book – enable organisations to build up distinctive and often complex combinations of abilities which make it possible to secure lasting competitive advantage. The development and growth of core competences is effectively supported by competence networks. They enable management to create centres of expertise on which to base new corporate abilities, and to establish competence centres which serve as integrators. Support is provided for platforms where employees with different competence profiles can meet. Competence networks also facilitate the establishment of such 'meeting places', where possibilities for 'disruptive' improvements which represent a qualitative leap forward can be filtered out and taken further. Links with strategic partners can be organised in a controlled fashion. Finally, the networks also facilitate the bringing together and the combining of core competences and abilities of two companies or organisations during mergers or takeovers.

Equipped with Competence for the Net Economy

Strategies which are surprising in their novelty, and thus initially considered disruptive, can be more easily developed and implemented by management if it can make use of a competence network. Top

management can introduce new guidelines for existing practices with lightning speed, intelligently exploiting these guidelines to achieve market dominance in a very short time-frame. This type of new strategy can also be used to do the impossible, so to speak, in organisational structures and processes. Major companies stand out on many fronts by implementing surprisingly novel strategies, whether through a change in the protected environment in which they operate, the effective communication of a new vision, the involvement and commitment of people with the company arranged as an extended enterprise, transforming the existing network of partnerships, or through new relationships, contents and processes. Throughout all this, competence networks provide effective information in a common infrastructure, within which new strategic concepts can be realised by involving people with very different minds.

Companies with established competence networks are generally better prepared than other companies for the entire complexity of e-Business and the demands of the Net economy. These companies successfully handle electronic communications as part of their daily routine, in a comprehensive manner.

This section about the most recent and far-reaching developments in knowledge management is not intended as a substitute for a manual on introducing this progressive management instrument. I have addressed the matter in some detail because it represents an instrument which both satisfies the demands of intelligent employees for new and more developed forms of collaboration and development of the individual's own skills, and is eminently suited to the demands of modern corporate structures, for example the extended enterprise. For that reason, I will conclude this point briefly with some consideration of the preconditions for successful working using this tool. Successful competence networks demand a combination of strategic, operational and system-specific qualities.

In terms of strategy, the targeted support of training and constant improvement in competences increase the value of the company. The company management needs to have a vision of the key competence domains and how they interact, as well as a clear management concept of the boundaries of the organisation and an understanding of its obligations in terms of providing the necessary resources.

In the operational areas, the significant aspects are the development of management for the competence domains and the clear commitment by top management to this extended knowledge management process, which needs to be continually maintained and developed. Naturally, this process extends over long time-frames.

For example, in the development of IT systems a key role is played by user interfaces which work effectively in delivering information flow for a particular individual. For the managers of the competence domain, there must be an assurance of comprehensive hardware and software support. An important condition is the inclusion of the regular information sources for the company. Controlled access and openness for third parties has been discussed earlier. Competence networks reach deep into the organisational structure of companies and bring about a shift in the inherited power relations; this must be accepted by the whole management at all levels. For that reason too, the introduction of such networks is a management issue at the highest level.

The expertise of individuals and the effective use of that expertise for the organisation are recognised today as the most important individual contribution which an employee can make. On the other hand, it must be fully apparent that the competence domains and their knowledge content are not the property of individual business units, but rank among the assets of the entire company, to which all units contribute and make use of. The effectiveness of the process can be measured above all in the form of its contributions to the important objectives of the organisation, and it can therefore only be assessed at the corporate level.

Specific Benefit for the Organisation

Every competence domain must deliver specific services with a recognisable strategic value for the organisation. The structure of such a network must reflect the most important existing and developing core competences, together with their constituent skills. Establishing a competence network with no clear strategic framework is a sure recipe for making mistakes.

Similar importance attaches to clear definition of the boundaries, since without this such a network is more dangerous than if no attempt is made

to establish such a network. Competence networks must be open to areas outside the company, because they are intended to cover the key contacts with the world beyond the company and therefore require input from third parties – whether these are suppliers, customers, specialised suppliers of content who supplement the company's own knowledge, or occasionally even competitors. Some domains are the result of a carefully considered collaboration, but on the other hand they should not provide unauthorised third parties with an opportunity to 'tap into' confidential knowledge and poach the company's own staff. The assets of the company which are bound up in competences must not be allowed to be softened up. Competence domains intended for collaboration with partners must be clearly defined and cleanly separated off from protected domains with confidential knowledge.

For every company, the development of a competence network demands considerable investment. Managers, members and the supporting units of the domains must invest their time. Information from external third parties costs money, as does the investment in suitable IT equipment and the related communications infrastructure and software. As indicated earlier, this all requires commitment over a long time-frame.

Self-organised communities are not sufficiently efficient for use in a professional context. For that reason, competence domains require committed management, whether by a lone specialist or group of specialists, who are familiar with the issue and who possess a profound understanding of the requirements and priorities for the organisation. In addition to this, they must have a good understanding of the importance of availability and the need for competence profiles – and they must know how to develop such profiles. Finally, those operating the domain must be willing to offer the whole organisation outstanding services.

Ultimately, it is important to arrange the competence domains as a 'one stop shop' where all the services and resources are brought together, since this is how to make them attractive to users. The synergy between external content and internal information generates outstanding knowledge, which is frequently the result of intensive interaction between competence-carriers. However, it is precisely this animated exchange which requires central management of a set of resources at the level of the competence domain. Another aspect of domain management

is extending explicit and individual invitations to members to join a competence domain, and to secure an agreement in writing with each individual member. This should involve the person involved and his or her management and the competence domain community, and the domain manager in particular. If a domain member does not satisfy expectations in terms of commitment and/or knowledge, then it must be possible to apply sanctions. The activities of domain members should be integrated into staff appraisal and staff development.

I have already mentioned that the switch from the traditional industrial manufacturing-based society to the modern service and knowledge society in Germany is being completed much more laboriously and slowly than in the USA, for example, because of our inherited ways of thinking. The importance of ideas as corporate drivers is demonstrated by US Internet companies such as AOL, Yahoo! or Amazon – even if one includes a suitable value adjustment to this assessment in recognition of the sometimes extreme overvaluations on the share market. Despite the transitory boom in dot-com valuations, Intershop and Pixelpark are examples confirming that the trend is not entirely unknown in Germany either. Today, corporate performance is frequently based on early recognition of trends and in bundling innovative opportunities, putting together quite different services to make them attractive to the market and to users; Microsoft is the best-known example of this. In publishing, this form of entrepreneurial activity has a long and proven tradition. Starting with the intellectual and/or artistic endeavour of the author, which must be recognised, assessed and translated into a commercial venture, the publisher co-ordinates such diverse business areas as manufacturing, marketing and sales in an interesting and exciting mix of cultural aspirations and commercial good sense.

Critical observers predict that the knowledge society will not break down the barriers within society, but will throw these into even more stark relief. To avoid a more marked divergence between rich and poor, between the unskilled and the skilled, as is threatened both in the industrialised and developing countries, determined counteractive measures are absolutely necessary, especially within the education system. Thus, for example, both Tony Blair and German Chancellor Gerhard Schröder have taken up the issue of the digital divide and set in motion appro-

priate Internet development programmes, comparable to the initiatives in Bavaria with 'Bayern-online'.[45] The critical levers are a lasting, improved and broadly based education, and the development of a service mentality which is above all lacking in Central Europe.

The meaningful communication of knowledge is, not least, a question of assembling knowledge in manageable portions – and offering it with effective methods of education. Life-long learning is not simply the prerogative of the new upper class, which Umberto Eco (in a deliberate echo of the former ruling class in the Soviet Union) terms the 'nomenklatura' and which he envisages as a broad layer of management. The writer and academic believes that in the industrialised countries new educational establishments will need to be developed, where in particular what will be taught is the ability to filter out the respective important and relevant information from among the mass of information.

Nevertheless, the rapidly expanding service sector, whose share of the employment market is set to rise to 68.7 per cent by 2010 (currently at 61.5 per cent), will also offer jobs for people with less developed intellectual abilities, despite the fact that the service society is in principle considerably more knowledge-based than the old manufacturing society. But someone making fresh waffles on a stall from morning till night does not need to have the full repertoire of knowledge enjoyed by the professional cake-maker, for example; simple mastery of a few manual operations, repeated many times, will be enough, along with a friendly personality and an awareness of personal hygiene. It is precisely jobs such as these which can make an effective contribution to avoiding the long-term unemployment of people who have only minimal opportunities in the employment markets of the high-wage countries, on account of their poor role models and limited abilities. In the service sector, however, they can play an active part in adding value. Having respect for people in such posts and for their worth as individuals is a challenge for social education programmes, and an area where Germans still need to catch up, since in Germany service is still mistakenly equated with subordination and obsequiousness.

However, the fact is that the so-called secondary services in research and development, organisation and management, together with consultancy, support, education and training, publicity and promotional work

offer the greatest opportunities for new jobs – although only for people with suitable training and a readiness to engage in life-long learning. There is no way of turning back on the road to the knowledge society, which will largely be a knowledge-based service society.

A major, comprehensive education and training offensive, which has long been called for by far-sighted politicians, must be started as soon as possible. When the government of the Netherlands took over the Presidency of the EU a number of years ago, it gave great weight to the issue of education and training in its programme for the future (see section 1.3). Booz Allen Hamilton was at that time much involved in the development of proposals for the programme. Today's universities with their ancient structures are clearly as little suited to the new demands as the institutions of the European Union – up until now, at any rate.

One only needs to look at the USA to see how many young companies are created out of the universities. Here in Germany, such knowledge-driven start-ups still provoke a furore: Aixtron in the area close to the Technical University of Aachen, IDS Scheer AG in close association with the University of Saarland in Saarbrücken, or the short-lived software and solutions provider BROKAT and the promising Internet companies freenet.de or Vocatus.de are still the rare exceptions to this attitude. However, the success of these companies could well encourage others to seek to emulate them. Academic work and entrepreneurial thinking create a fruitful symbiosis in such instances – which, regrettably, occurs far more frequently in the USA than in Germany, Austria or Switzerland, where inherited (one might also say, ossified) concepts of the role of the university teacher often stifle at birth initiatives which could otherwise be entertained.

It goes without saying that this education and training offensive should not only be implemented at university level, but must include all levels and areas of education from the primary school onward. Information technology companies, in particular, have set up a large number of initiatives over recent years to fully equip schools with computers and provide them with a connection to the Internet. Bavaria has run and is currently running model initiatives to better prepare schools and teachers for the educational requirements of the information society.

Top Management Must Make a Visible Commitment

As stated above, only if this commitment is visible can competence networks grow, and expand in harmony with the needs of the whole company by being supported and used by all business units. They can then also develop to become an integral part of strategic planning and strategic change.

Naturally the issue also presents a number of further aspects, the social aspect being of particular importance. In that regard, it must be clear to all those involved that even the most intelligent, high-performance network cannot replace the interpersonal exchange, but it can be an effective supplement to that exchange and make it more efficient. If a domain is well managed, then it produces interesting opportunities to improve the co-existence and collaboration of employees in the social community constituted by the company. After all, communities of experts do not exclude the possibility of a sense of solidarity and a reciprocal relationship of trust. On the contrary, it is actually these 'old-fashioned' virtues which form the basis for successful co-existence in a domain. I have already quoted the observation by Professor Dr Frieder Meyer-Krahmer that for employees who are prepared to perform, identification with individual projects will be more important than identification with the whole company, and provides them with a source of motivation. This observation can also apply to the role of the competence-carrier in the domain.

Turning towards the value and management of knowledge is only one of the many responses which management must make to the challenges of the present and the future. The starting point for management seeking lasting success, however, is a whole set of fundamental insights, which without exception are determined by the merciless dictates of permanent change. These are insights into the following:

- The role of the individual in the modern, knowledge-based, market-driven and customer-oriented company;

- The changed duties of the CEO at the head of the global core with a flat hierarchy and a flexible, project-oriented organisation with considerable independence and autonomy of the local/regional units;

- The importance of creativity and the readiness to take risks, which can only develop in an open culture which takes the individual seriously in terms of individuality and originality;

- The need to make available risk capital for young companies, with a new readiness to accept controlled risk and using new capital market instruments, enabling those companies to bring on those innovations which a large, 'old' organisation often cannot develop, or does so too late;

- The status of the knowledge located in individuals and transferred to competence domains as a critical success factor.

None of these ideas are developed in the sterile world of the theoretician far removed from the company, but are logical consequences of the major, revolutionary changes in the conditions governing economic activity at the start of the third millennium, to which the first part of this book is devoted.

e-Commerce as an Impulse for Development

There are hundreds of excellent examples to show how e-Commerce is being used in Germany intelligently and comprehensively. This book does not have sufficient scope to address this aspect fully. Four examples will have to suffice, which nevertheless demonstrate the general trends:

- As an example of the new forms of use of the Internet, one might consider new car catalogues, started with data about the widest possible range of vehicles and actively used by manufacturers such as VW, Audi and Toyota. In the first stage, potential buyers can make an initial selection using the criteria of price, performance and fuel consumption. The selected car can then be equipped with extras on screen. The online specification is then forwarded to the connected dealer. For financing, the online user has the option of approaching almost any bank with a computer-based operation. And a free valuation is given for the car which one currently drives. One important

feature of this approach is that the conventional sales channel is left largely intact.

- An unusual example is an online magazine put together by international consumer protection organisations and especially aimed at young people. The site has been put together by 200 young people from five European countries. They swap experiences about buying clothes, leisure, sports and music – frankly and openly, as you would expect with young people. The aim is to liberate self-regulating powers using the Internet.

- A different approach – which similarly aims at securing advantages for consumers and which, even if it has yet to enjoy lasting commercial success, demonstrates how the Internet intensifies competition and calls into question traditional sales channels and forms – is the concept of Letsbuyit.com which has been taken over from the USA. Online users bundle their demands for a particular product to generate volumes of orders which can be used to secure a high discount. Any member can establish a buying group. The more people interested in buying that product who come together, the more favourable the terms for the purchase secured by each individual. The principle speculates on changed consumer behaviour. Whether the business idea is sufficiently attractive for the long term will be shown by the market.

- Recently, the company Vocatus AG was launched to pursue a noteworthy business idea. Vocatus aims to be Europe's leading independent forum for praise, complaints and suggestions for improvements from consumers about products and services. The company evaluates the numerous consumer opinions being submitted via the Internet and communicates these in a structured format to the companies and institutions concerned. In other words, it operates a highly modern form of current market and opinion research – on the one hand as a basis for rapidly responsive complaints management, and on the other as an instrument for better customer orientation, thanks to the significantly heightened knowledge of customers. Collaboration with leading opinion researchers ensures the academic quality of this new service. Customers also get to know the opinions of other consumers.

The above examples illustrate the most important megatrends of the present:

- New sales channels are revolutionising sales and brand management.
- The distribution of power in the markets is shifting in favour of the customer.
- The competition is becoming more intensive in every aspect.
- The speed of economic processes is increasing dramatically.
- Companies are networking more and more as extended enterprises.

The differential return on being the first and fastest in the market will be greater than before, thanks to the I-World, because that return can be obtained via the Internet quickly and relatively cost-effectively from a wide market presence, which instantly attracts attention across regions and indeed worldwide. Earlier, it was quite possible to be the first to market in one's own region, but no-one else in the wider environment knew about it. Success necessarily remained limited where limited use was made of advertising media. The reverse side of the coin is that competitors are quickly on the same trail, because business successes on the Internet do not go unnoticed.

Globalisation Presupposes Networking

Economists tend to see globalisation as a central force (although it can only function on the basis of global information systems, in other words using new technologies), whereas it might be the case that these technologies would not have developed without the concrete and pressing needs of a globally networked world. However, there can be no doubt that globalisation has had its biggest practical effects on the need for change in companies. It represents the biggest challenge to their ability and readiness to adapt to changed conditions or go under. Change management has become part of business culture under these conditions.

In this regard, it is interesting to consider how globalisation is presented in the opinion of major companies.

Operating Globally Means ...

At the turn of the year 1999/2000, leading German companies were asked in a survey[44] what they understood by globalisation and what strategies they were pursuing in that regard. The responses are unsurprising, but the tone which they set correlates interestingly with the assertions made in this book.

For BASF, which established a branch in New York as early as 1873, globalisation is 'nothing new':

> However, what is new is the scope and the speed of the international networking of knowledge, goods, information and capital. A company which, like ourselves, is aspiring to rank among the successful companies in its sector in the future cannot set itself against this trend, but must actively engage in shaping the direction of that trend.

Bayer sees its own corporate network as the basis for exploiting the major opportunities:

> By globalisation, we mean first and foremost the increasing worldwide networking of markets. The basis for this development is on the one hand technological progress, and on the other the political, economic and social growing together of continents, countries and cultures. Our strategy is to exploit the major opportunities arising out of globalisation by developing a suitable network within our company, extending across all functions from research through to sales.

In its response, DaimlerChrysler formulates a core phrase of the philosophy of globalisation:

> Being global means not only selling products in many markets, but also developing and manufacturing products in many markets. Via the network of supply channels and the transfer of expertise which this facilitates, the company also derives positive effects in its home market.

Adidas Salomon expands this thinking to include the cultural aspect:

Global alignment also means being represented through subsidiaries in the most important world markets and employing workers with the widest variety of nationalities and cultural backgrounds. This all supports the attitude of being open to the world, which is in turn the basis for worldwide market success.

In its assessment of globalisation, Fresenius Medical Care (FMC) places an emphasis on competitive orientation:

Globalisation brings about an increasingly competitively oriented environment, focused on serving customers even more effectively and efficiently. As one of the most important components in the globalisation process, technology has contributed to creating markets which are active all around the world, 24 hours a day, 365 days a year.

SAP makes reference to the aspect relating to the employment market in its response:

It is not about moving jobs to countries elsewhere on grounds of cost, but – and this is far more essential– about being able to handle new requirements. The old concept of national companies geared up to export products has been superseded. Today, every company must be as close to its customers as possible with its products and solutions. The company which yesterday simply exported its goods and services must today offer all the services which its customers are expecting everywhere in the world, and offer them locally and on a global basis.

The diversity of these answers from globally oriented companies reflects in exemplary fashion the complexity of the challenges and management tasks which necessarily arise as a result of globalisation. Top management can only meet these demands with a hope of lasting success if it gives to its most valuable, scarce resource, the individuals within the company, that central role which I have considered in each of the preceding chapters by looking at relevant situations found in practice.

The World plc as a Mutation in the Orders of Magnitude

In a lecture to top managers in the German economy, Konradin Herdt took issue with the effects of globalisation on the social market economy:

> Ultimately, it is not the fundamental rules of operation of the social market economy which have changed, but the scale on which they are being played out. And this mutation in the orders of magnitude is so violent that it also reaches down to the very roots of policy thinking on orders of magnitude and appears to be jointly responsible for the fact that in Germany the social market economy is even experiencing problems of acceptance ten years after its triumph over the socialist central command economy. Looking to the future, we must ask ourselves whether capitalism is to be kept in balance in such a way that it does not destroy itself or degenerate in some other way. That would indeed be the case if nothing were to develop from below to take things forward and at the senior level there were only a one-way street leading to persistent concentration. But with increasing size there is no lessening of entrepreneurial risk. Rather, the potential for risk multiplies. And '*big* is *beautiful*' only holds true if it is simultaneously the case that '*small* is *beautiful*' – in other words, if the entrepreneurial economy repeatedly renews itself through start-ups and through the SME sector. [5]

'Ultimately All Problems in the Economy are People-related'

The starting position is practically identical in all industrialised countries. Companies can only compete in this global environment if they have the better, more flexible, highly motivated employees. The influence of e-Business and the Internet is intensifying the competition for able employees. The banker Alfred Herrhausen summarised his experiences thus: 'Ultimately all problems in the economy are people-related.' Transferred to the context of company management, this means that personnel management is a critically important issue. In this book I have attempted to make clear that the people factor is the universal key to overcoming almost all corporate challenges, since most of these challenges derive from how people in the company are handled.

The Individual is the Key

It is self-evident that in a new business model such as that developed by Booz Allen Hamilton with the centreless corporation,[19] the personnel strategy plays a central role in securing growth and prosperity for the company; it is a strategy which can no longer solely be directed towards filling posts, but must instead be aimed at investing in people.

To implement this new personnel strategy, three steps are required:

- The personnel strategy must be consistently aligned with the corporate vision and must be tailored to the individual company.

- Only co-existence in partnerships can reduce the requirements of the company and all the needs of employees to a common denominator in the form of a new ethical contract, which is no longer based on unbreakable loyalty to the company and a guarantee of life-long employment.

- The organisation must be focused on those critical processes in handling people which drive forward success. In other words, a personnel strategy will only enjoy success today and tomorrow if it integrates the needs, entitlements and problems of employees. Loyalty can only develop and grow in an atmosphere where satisfaction and motivation thrive.

Performance – both in terms of the specialism and on a personal level – must be at the forefront of all strategic measures relating to staff. However, that also means that deficient performance must have consequences or must ultimately result in being ejected from the company.

The new mobility brought about by the age of globalisation, the I-World as a synonym for worldwide networking and the key to a virtual universe which causes spatial distances to collapse, the advantages of competition freed from monopolistic chains, benefiting the consumer most obviously in the field of communications – these are all changes with direct relevance for people on the way from the industrial society to the knowledge society, with its vastly increased demands for intellectual, mental and physical mobility and flexibility.

7 Golden Rules

For companies which seek to do justice to the people factor and thus address the challenges of constant change, '7 golden rules' summarise:

1. Corporate action must be based on a clear, simple system of values. These values must be lived out. That creates a new form of loyalty. Common objectives and a common cultural understanding of values will be important for the continuity of corporate development, as this continuity is no longer guaranteed by the CEO's long-term tenure in office.

2. The entrepreneurial personality achieves impact through being a role model. The increasing complexity of the parameters with relevance to decision-making, and the growing time pressure and competitive pressure in the age of globalisation and the I-World, demand entrepreneurial leadership figures with character, education and life knowledge, out of which social competence is developed. Being a role model presupposes consistency in one's thinking and actions just as much as the ability to encourage and support followers.

3. The development of an all-pervasive culture of customer orientation, extending from the CEO right through to the trainee, is vital for survival. In achieving this, the company transforms itself from being technology-driven to being market-driven and 'people-oriented'.

4. Companies must invest in the individual, in his or her abilities and knowledge. They must be aware of the asset of knowledge, and not simply fit people to positions, that is, they must not obstruct initiative, but encourage it. Continuously updated competence has a greater status than the guarantee of life-long employment, which has long since become obsolete.

5. Networking using competence networking, while demonstrating flexibility, flat hierarchies and project orientation, is the distinguishing feature of the organisational form appropriate to the era of globalisation and the I-World.

6. Success management with a high degree of autonomy at all levels of decision-making is based on transparency and openness. Only then will change be understood, accepted and actively driven forward.

7. Managers must provide the individuals within the company with space for creativity, originality and a readiness to take risks, for example in project teams which cut across hierarchies. Creativity can only thrive in an atmosphere of freedom. Then – in destructured and debureaucratised spaces – initiatives lead to innovations.

The readiness to change must not remain limited to top management and the second tier of management; it must include all employees. That can only happen if the individuals within the company are perceived, respected and encouraged as people with their own identity, creativity and originality. This compels all successful companies to re-evaluate the individual as the carrier of knowledge and source of creativity, and as the driver of change. Therefore companies need forms of organisation which operate more like living human organisms.

Notes

1. Lay, Professor Dr Rupert: *Führen durch das Wort: Motivation – Kommunikation – Praktische Führungsdialektik.* Econ & List Taschenbuchverlag, München, 1999.
2. Rommel, Manfred: Dissensgespräche. *Börsen-Zeitung,*15.01.1999.
3. Schrempp, Jürgen E.: 'Die Kernelemente des Kapitalismus bedeuten nicht den Kampf aller gegen alle'. *Die Welt,* 12.7.1999.
4. Schwarzkopf, H. Norman: *Man muss kein Held sein.* C. Bertelsmann, München, 1992 (published in English as *It Doesn't Take a Hero: The Autobiography of General H. Norman Schwarzkopf,* Bantam Books, New York, 1993).
5. Herdt, Hans Konradin: 'Welt AG und soziale Marktwirtschaft'. *Börsen-Zeitung,* 04.9.1999.
6. Wittkemper, Dr Gerd and Künstner, Thomas: 'i World – Das Internet verändert die globale Wirtschaft'. *Bayerischer Monatsspiegel,* 2/1999.
7. Booz Allen Hamilton: 'Enabling the Information Society', Study for the Dutch Economics Ministry, Den Haag, 1997.
8. Fara, Dr Leopold K.: 'Wissen ist Macht, wenn alle es wissen'. *Die Welt,* 16 August 1999.
9. Meyer-Krahmer, Professor Dr Frieder in 'Die Kunst, dem Neuen den Weg zu ebnen' interview, summary (*VDI-Nachrichten*). Special publication to mark 50 years of the Fraunhofer-Gesellschaft, 1999.
10. Höhler, Professor Dr Gertrud: quoted in translation from *Die Zukunftsgesellschaft.* Econ Verlag, Düsseldorf, 1986.
11. Warnecke, Professor Dr Hans-Jürgen: 'Die Kunst, dem Neuen den Weg zu ebnen', interview, summary (*VDI-Nachrichten*). Special publication to mark 50 years of the Fraunhofer-Gesellschaft, 1999.
12. Postman, Neil: quoted in translation from *Wir amüsieren uns zu Tode: Urteilsbildung im Zeitalter der Unterhaltungsindustrie.* S. Fischer, Frankfurt am Main, 1985 (published in English as *Amusing Ourselves to Death.* Methuen, London, 1987).
13. Glotz Peter, Süssmuth, Rita and Seitz, Konrad: quoted in translation from *Die planlosen Eliten: Versäumen wir Deutschen die Zukunft?* Edition Ferenczy bei Bruckmann, München, 1992.
14. Walter, Professor Dr Norbert: 'Fehlt den global operierenden Karrieristen die soziale Kompetenz?' *VDI-Nachrichten,* 07.1.2000.
15. Horx, Matthias: 'Willkommen im Jahrhundert der neuen Nomaden'. *Die Welt,* 30.12.1999.

16. Wiegran, Gaby and Koth, Hardy: quoted in translation from *firma.nach.maß – Erfolgreiches E-Business mit individuellen Produkten, Preisen und Profilen*. Financial Times/Prentice Hall, München, 2000 (published in English as *The Custom Enterprise.com*. F/T.COM).

17. Pohle, Klaus, in: 'Scherings Powerstrategie soll Kurs beflügeln'. *Börsen-Zeitung*, 11.11.1999.

18. Gonschorrek, Ulrich and Norbert: *Management Praxis von A bis Z – Leitfaden durch die aktuellen Managementkonzepte*. F.A.Z. Verlagsbereich Buch, Frankfurt am Main, 1999.

19. Pasternack, Bruce A.: *The Centerless Corporation: A New Model for Transforming Your Organization for Growth and Prosperity*. Simon & Schuster, New York, 1998.

20. Franch, Josep and Kashani, Kamran: 'Der Aufstieg des internationalen Managers'. *Handelsblatt*, 1.7.1999.

21. Welch, Jack, in *Manager Magazin*, 8/1996.

22. Goeudevert, Daniel: 'Großkonzerne müssen wie Familienunternehmen geführt werden'. *Die Welt*, 13.9.1999.

23. Grove, Andy, in *Manager Magazin*, 11/1999.

24. Plattner, Hasso: 'Erst vernetzte virtuelle Unternehmen'. *FAZ*, 16.11.1999.

25. Ungeheuer, Udo, in: 'Wie sich Schott seine Zukunft sichert'. *VDI-Nachrichten*, 10.12.1999.

26. Wiedeking, Wendelin, interview in *Manager Magazin*, 3/1999.

27. Rappaport, Professor Alfred, in: 'Über den Shareholder Value hinaus'. *FAZ*, 23.8.1999.

28. Maucher, Helmut, (at that time head of Nestlé AG) in *Die Welt*, 23.9.1999.

29. Philips, Frits: *Ein Leben mit Philips*. Seewald, Stuttgart, 1979.

30. Glotz, Professor Dr Peter: 'Wir brauchen Exzellenz und Internationalität', interview in *Die Welt*, 25.8.1999.

31. Lauda, Niki, interview in the *Welt am Sonntag*, No. 40/1999.

32. Bozem, Dr Karlheinz in an interview with the author.

33. Lay, Professor Dr Rupert, interview in *RAG – Das Magazin*, 1999.

34. Noelle-Neumann, Professor Dr Elisabeth, in *FAZ*, 2.11.1999.

35. Sennett, Richard: quoted in translation from *Der flexible Mensch: Die Kultur des neuen Kapitalismus*. Berlin Verlag, Berlin, 1999 (published in English as *The Corrosion of Character: The Personal Consequences of Work in the New Capitalism*. WW Norton, London, 1998).

36. Bossers, Cornelis im Vorwort zu *Rembrandt: Hundert Radierungen*. Hamburger Kunsthalle, 1987.

37. Bernhardt, Dr Wolfgang: 'Übernahmen und Fusionen sind weder Allheilmittel noch Versicherung auf dem Weg in die unternehmerische Zukunft'. *FAZ*, 18.6.1999.

38. Coureil, Pierre: quoted in translation from *Mehrwert: Die neue Aufgabe der Führung*. Campus, Frankfurt am Main, 1999.

39. Wellershoff, Klaus, in *Die Welt*, 18.1.2000.

40. O'Toole, James: *Leading Change*. Jossey-Bass, San Francisco, 1995.

41. Powell, Marc and Jaruzelski, Barry: 'Wachstum managen – Vitalisierung durch Innovationsmanagement' in *Unternehmensvitalisierung*. Schäffer-Poeschel, Stuttgart, 1997.

42. Lupenberger, Dirk R., in: 'Siemens gibt Starthilfe'. *Welt am Sonntag*, 06.2.2000.

43. Remmel, Manfred, in: 'Eine negative Risikowahrnehmung führt zu verpassten Chancen'. *FAZ*, 27.9.1999.

44. 'Deutsche Konzerne betonen globale Präsenz'. Survey in *Börsen-Zeitung*, Frankfurt am Main, 31.12.1999.

45. Booz Allen Hamilton brochures: 'Achieving Universal Access – Internet Policy Recommendations to the UK Government', April 2000 and 'Digitale Spaltung in Deutschland – Ausgangssituation, Internationaler Vergleich, Handlungsempfehlungen', August 2000.
46. Kirchner, Dr Baldur: quoted in translation from *Sprechen vor Gruppen*. Ernst Klett, Stuttgart, 1980.
47. Herdt, Hans Konradin and Schmidt, Albrecht in *Börsen-Zeitung* 30.6.1999.
48. O'Toole, James: quoted from a lecture 10/96.
49. Forrester Research: 'eBusiness Strategy Needs Help', February 2000.
50. Habermas, Jürgen: quoted in translation from *Strukturwandel der Öffentlichkeit*. Suhrkamp, 1990 (originally post-doctoral thesis, University of Marburg 1961) (published in English as *The Structural Change of the Public Sphere*. Cambridge, MA: MIT Press, 1989).
51. Mertius, Kai, Heisig, Peter and Vorbeck, Jens: quoted in translation from *Knowledge Management*. Springer, 2001.
52. Lay, Professor Dr Rupert: Interview in *io management*, 6/2000.
53. Breuer, Rolf-Ernst, in: 'Die Aktivitäten von Deutscher und Dresdner Bank im Fokus'. *Börsen-Zeitung*, 09.3.2000.
54. Booz Allen Hamilton: '10 Erfolgsfaktoren im e-business'. FAZ Institut Frankfurt, 2000.
55. Otto, Dr Michael, in: 'Presse-News vom 29.März 2000'. www.otto.de.
56. Chambers, John T. in an interview with Booz Allen Hamilton.
57. Krömker, Dr Heidi, in: 'Die Kunst der Einfachheit'. *Forschung und Innovation* 2/1999.

INDEX